SIDE by SIDE

SECOND EDITION

BOOK 3

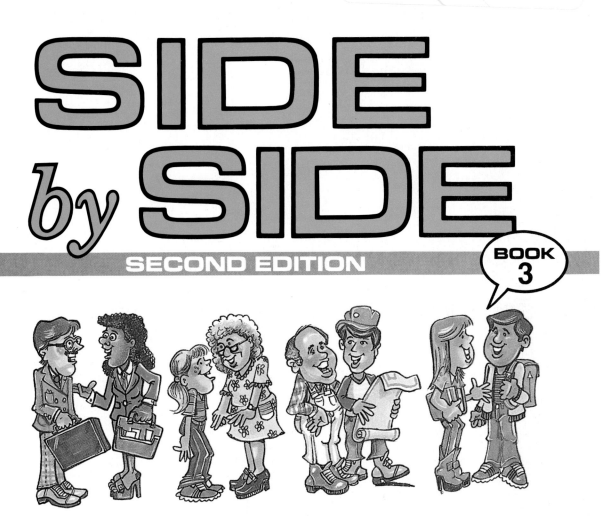

Steven J. Molinsky / Bill Bliss

PRENTICE HALL REGENTS
Englewood Cliffs, New Jersey 07632

Library of Congress Cataloging-in-Publication Data

Molinsky, Steven J.
  Side by side.

  Includes indexes.
   1. English language—Conversation and phrase books.
2. English language—Textbooks for foreign speakers.
I. Bliss, Bill. II. Title.
PE1131.M58 1989   428.3'4   88-22455
ISBN 0-13-811076-X (v. 1)
ISBN 0-13-811241-X (v. 2)
ISBN 0-13-811761-6 (v. 3)

Editorial/production supervision: Janet Johnston
Art supervision: Karen Salzbach
Manufacturing buyer: Laura Crossland
Cover design: Kenny Beck

Illustrated by Richard E. Hill

© 1989 by Prentice Hall Regents
Prentice-Hall, Inc.
A Paramount Communications Company
Englewood Cliffs, New Jersey 07632

Printed in the United States of America

10 9 8 7 6 5 4 3 2

ISBN 0-13-467812-5

Prentice-Hall International (UK) Limited, *London*
Prentice-Hall of Australia Pty. Limited, *Sydney*
Prentice-Hall Canada Inc., *Toronto*
Prentice-Hall Hispanoamericana, S.A., *Mexico*
Prentice-Hall of India Private Limited, *New Delhi*
Prentice-Hall of Japan, Inc., *Tokyo*
Simon & Schuster Asia Pte. Ltd., *Singapore*
Editora Prentice-Hall do Brasil, Ltda., *Rio de Janeiro*

CONTENTS

Review:
- Simple Present Tense ■
- Present Continuous Tense ■
- Subject Pronouns ■
- Object Pronouns ■
- Possessive Adjectives ■

They're Busy

(I am)	I'm				
(He is)	He's				
(She is)	She's	} eating.			
(It is)	It's				
(We are)	We're				
(You are)	You're	}			
(They are)	They're				

Am	I
Is	{ he / she / it } eating?
Are	{ we / you / they }

	I	am.
Yes,	{ he / she / it }	is.
	{ we / you / they }	are.

A. Are you busy?

B. Yes, I am. I'm studying.

A. What are you studying?

B. I'm studying English.

1. Is Helen busy?
cooking spaghetti

2. Is Tom busy?
reading the newspaper

3. Are Bobby and Judy busy?
studying mathematics

4. Are you busy?
typing a letter

5. Are you and your brother busy?
cleaning the basement

6. Is Jane busy?
knitting a sweater

7. Are Mr. and Mrs. Watson busy?
baking cookies

8. Is Beethoven busy?
composing a new symphony

9. Is Whistler busy?
painting a portrait of his mother

What Are They Doing?

| I
We
You
They } eat. | Do { I
we
you
they } | eat? |
| He
She
It } eats. | Does { he
she
it } | |

| Yes, | I
we
you
they } do. |
| | he
she
it } does. |

A. What are you doing?

B. I'm practicing the piano.

A. Do you practice the piano very often?

B. Yes, I do. I practice the piano whenever I can.

1. What's Edward doing?
bake bread

2. What's Janet doing?
swim

3. What are Mr. and Mrs. Green doing?
clean their apartment

4. What are you doing?
read Shakespeare

5. What are you and your friend doing?
study English

6. What's Mary doing?
write to her grandparents

7. What's your neighbor doing?
play baseball with his son

8. What are Mr. and Mrs. Baker doing?
do aerobics

9.

Do You Like to Ski?

No, $\left\{\begin{array}{l} \text{I} \\ \text{we} \\ \text{you} \\ \text{they} \end{array}\right\}$ don't. (do not)		
$\left\{\begin{array}{l} \text{he} \\ \text{she} \\ \text{it} \end{array}\right\}$ doesn't. (does not)		

I'm not. (am not)
No, $\left\{\begin{array}{l} \text{he} \\ \text{she} \\ \text{it} \end{array}\right\}$ isn't. (is not)
$\left\{\begin{array}{l} \text{we} \\ \text{you} \\ \text{they} \end{array}\right\}$ aren't. (are not)

A. Do you like to ski?

B. No, I don't. I'm not a very good skier.

1. Does Jim like to dance?

dancer

2. Does Rita like to sing?

singer

3. Do Mr. and Mrs. Brown like to skate?

skaters

4. Do you like to type?

typist

5. Do you and your friend like to play tennis?

tennis players

6. Does Shirley like to swim?

swimmer

7. Does David like to study?

student

8. Do you like to play sports?

athlete

9. Does Marvin like to cook?

cook

PRACTICING

My sisters, my brother, and I are busy this afternoon. We're staying after school, and we're practicing different things.

I'm practicing tennis. I practice tennis every day after school. My tennis coach tells me I'm an excellent tennis player, and my friends tell me I play tennis better than anyone else in the school. I want to be a professional tennis player when I grow up. That's why I practice every day.

My brother Jimmy is practicing football. He practices football every day after school. His football coach tells him he's an excellent football player, and his friends tell him he plays football better than anyone else in the school. Jimmy wants to be a professional football player when he grows up. That's why he practices every day.

My sister Susan is practicing the violin. She practices the violin every day after school. Her music teacher tells her she's an excellent violinist, and her friends tell her she plays the violin better than anyone else in the school. Susan wants to be a professional violinist when she grows up. That's why she practices every day.

My sisters Patty and Melissa are practicing ballet. They practice ballet every day after school. Their dance teacher tells them they're excellent ballet dancers, and their friends tell them they dance ballet better than anyone else in the school. Patty and Melissa want to be professional ballet dancers when they grow up. That's why they practice every day.

CHECK-UP

Q & A

You're talking with the person who told the story on page 5. Using this model, create dialogs based on the story.

A. What's *your brother Jimmy* doing?
B. *He's* practicing *football*.
A. *Does he* practice very often?
B. Yes, *he does. He practices* every day after school.
A. *Is he* a good *football player*?
B. Yes, *he is. His football coach* says *he's* excellent, and *his* friends tell *him he plays football* better than anyone else in the school.

Listening

Listen and choose the best answer.

1. a. I practice the piano.
   b. I'm practicing the piano.

2. a. Yes, I am.
   b. Yes, I do.

3. a. Yes, I am.
   b. Yes, I do.

4. a. He cooks dinner.
   b. He's cooking dinner.

5. a. My husband cooks.
   b. My husband is cooking.

6. a. No, they aren't.
   b. No, they don't.

7. a. Yes, when he grows up.
   b. Yes, when she grows up.

8. a. Yes, you are.
   b. Yes, we are.

9. a. Yes. She's a very good singer.
   b. Yes. She's a very good swimmer.

10. a. He's reading the newspaper.
    b. He's eating spaghetti.

IN YOUR OWN WORDS

For Writing and Discussion

Tell about studying English.

Do you go to English class? Where?
When do you go to class?
What's your teacher's name?
Do you practice English after class?
  How do you practice?
  Who do you practice with?

How Often?

I	my	me
he	his	him
she	her	her
it	its	it
we	our	us
you	your	you
they	their	them

A. Who are you calling?

B. **I'm** calling **my** brother in Chicago.

A. How often do you call **him**?

B. I call **him** every Sunday evening.*

A. What are George and Herman talking about?

B. **They're** talking about **their** grandchildren.

A. How often do they talk about **them**?

B. They talk about **them** all the time.*

*You can also say:
every day, week, weekend, month, year
every morning, afternoon, evening, night
every Sunday, Monday, . . . January, February, . . .

once a
twice a
three times a
four times a
⋮
all the time

} day, week, month, year

7

1. Who is Mrs. Lopez calling?
daughter in San Francisco

2. Who are you writing to?
uncle

3. Who is Walter visiting?
neighbors across the street

4. Who is Mrs. Morgan writing to?
son in the army

5. Who is Mr. Davis arguing with?
landlord

6. What are the students talking about?
teachers

7. What are you complaining about?
electric bill

8. Who is Mr. Crabapple shouting at?
employees

9. Who is Little Red Riding Hood visiting?
grandmother

10.

8

ON YOUR OWN: Getting to Know Each Other

1. **Tell the class about yourself. Answer these questions and then ask other students:**

   Where are you from?
   Where do you live now?
   What do you do? (I'm a mechanic, a student...)
   Where do you work/study?

2. **Talk about the people in your family and ask other students about their families:**

   Are you married? Are you single?
   Do you live with your parents? Do you live alone?

3. **Tell the class about your _____ [husband, wife, children, parents, brother(s), sister(s) . . .]:**

   What are their names?
   How old are they?
   Where do they live?
   What do they do? Where?

4. **Tell the class about your interests and ask other students about theirs:**

   What do you like to do in your free time?
   Do you like to play sports? Which? How often?
   How often do you watch TV? read? listen to music?

GRAMMAR

Present Continuous Tense

(I am)	I'm	
(He is) (She is) (It is)	He's She's It's	eating.
(We are) (You are) (They are)	We're You're They're	

Am	I	
Is	he she it	eating?
Are	we you they	

To Be: Short Answers

	I	am.
Yes,	he she it	is.
	we you they	are.

	I'm	not.
No,	he she it	isn't.
	we you they	aren't.

Simple Present Tense

I We You They	eat.
He She It	eats.

Do	I we you they	eat?
Does	he she it	

Yes,	I we you they	do.
	he she it	does.

No,	I we you they	don't.
	he she it	doesn't.

Subject Pronouns	Possessive Adjectives	Object Pronouns
I	my	me
he	his	him
she	her	her
it	its	it
we	our	us
you	your	you
they	their	them

FUNCTIONS

Asking for and Reporting Information

Are you busy?
  Yes, I am. I'm *studying*.
What are you *studying*?
  I'm *studying English*.

Who are you calling?

What are you doing?
  I'm *practicing the piano*.

What *are George and Herman* talking about?

What *are you* complaining about?

What's *your teacher's* name?
What are their names?

What do you do?

When do you *go to class*?

Where are you from?
Where do you live now?
Where do you *work*?

How old *are they*?

How often do you *watch TV*?

Do you *practice* very often?
  Yes, I do.

Is *he* a good *football player*?
  Yes, *he* is.

Are you married?
Are you single?

Do you live with *your parents*?
Do you live *alone*?

His football coach says *he's*
  excellent.
His friends tell *him he plays*
  football better than anyone else.

Inquiring about Likes/Dislikes

Do you like to *ski*?

What do you like to do *in your free
  time*?

Expressing Inability

I'm not a very good *skier*.

Review:
Simple Past Tense
(Regular and Irregular
Verbs) ▪
Past Continuous Tense ▪

Did They Sleep Well Last Night?

What did
{ I
he
she
it
we
you
they }
do?

I
He
She
It
We
You
They }
worked.

I
He
She
It }
was

We
You
They }
were
tired.

A. Did Henry sleep well last night?

B. Yes, he did. He was VERY tired.

A. Why? What did he do yesterday?

B. He **cleaned his apartment** all day.

1. *you*
   study English

2. *Gloria*
   work hard

3. *David and Jeff*
   wash windows

4. *Miss Henderson*
   teach

5. *Mr. and Mrs. Warren*
   look for an apartment

6. *Jack*
   ride his bicycle

7. *Irene*
   write letters

8. *the President*
   meet important people

9. _____

Did Mrs. Clark Shout at Her Son?

I	
He	
She	
It	} did/didn't
We	(did not)
You	
They	

I	
He	was/wasn't
She	(was not)
It	

We	were/weren't
You	(were not)
They	

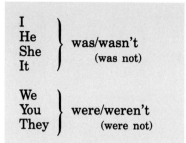

A. Did Mrs. Clark shout at her son?
B. Yes, she did. She was angry.

A. Did Sam do well on his exam?
B. No, he didn't. He wasn't prepared.

1. Did Marylou cry a lot when her dog ran away?
   Yes, _____. _____ upset.

2. Did Katherine sleep well last night?
   No, _____. _____ tired.

3. Did you fall asleep during the lecture?
   Yes, _____. _____ bored.

4. Did Mr. and Mrs. Mason finish their dinner last night?
   No, _____. _____ hungry.

5. Did Gregory forget his lines during the school play?
   Yes, _____. _____ nervous.

6. Did they have anything to drink after dinner last night?
   No, _____. _____ thirsty.

7. Did Tommy cover his eyes during the science fiction movie?
   Yes, _____. _____ scared.

8. Did George and his brother leave on the two o'clock train?
   No, _____. _____ on time.

How Did John Break His Arm?

I		
He	} was	
She		
It		
		working.
We		
You	} were	
They		

A. How did John break his arm?

B. He broke it while he was **playing tennis**.

1. How did Sally break her leg?
ski down a mountain

2. How did Martin lose his wallet?
play baseball with his son

3. How did Peggy meet her husband?
read in the library one day

4. How did Mr. and Mrs. Thompson burn themselves?
bake cookies

5. How did Walter cut himself?
shave

6. How did Alan get a black eye?
argue with his neighbor

7. How did Martha cut herself?
prepare dinner

8. How did Rita rip her pants?
do her daily exercises

9. How did Fred meet his wife?
wait for the bus one day

10. How did Presto the Magician hurt himself?

practice a new magic trick

How about YOU?

How did you meet your (husband, wife, boyfriend, girlfriend, best friend)?
    Where were you?
    What were you doing?
    What was he/she doing?

DIFFICULT EXPERIENCES

Miss Henderson usually teaches very well, but she didn't teach very well this morning. In fact, she taught very badly. While she was teaching, her supervisor was sitting at the back of the room and watching her. It was a very difficult experience for Miss Henderson. She realized she wasn't teaching very well, but she couldn't do anything about it. She was too nervous.

Stuart usually types very well, but he didn't type very well today. In fact, he typed very badly. While he was typing, his boss was standing behind him and looking over his shoulder. It was a difficult experience for Stuart. He realized he wasn't typing very well, but he couldn't do anything about it. He was too upset.

The Johnson Brothers usually sing very well, but they didn't sing very well last night. In fact, they sang very badly. While they were singing, their parents were sitting in the audience and waving at them. It was a difficult experience for the Johnson Brothers. They realized they weren't singing very well, but they couldn't do anything about it. They were too embarrassed.

The President usually speaks very well, but he didn't speak very well this afternoon. In fact, he spoke very badly. While he was speaking, several demonstrators were standing at the back of the room and shouting at him. It was a difficult experience for the President. He realized he wasn't speaking very well, but he couldn't do anything about it. He was too angry.

✔CHECK-UP

Q & A

Miss Henderson, Stuart, the Johnson Brothers, and the President are talking with friends about their difficult experiences. Using this model, create dialogs based on the story on page 16.

A. You know...*I* didn't *teach* very well *this morning.*
B. You didn't?
A. No. In fact, *I taught* very badly.
B. I don't understand. You usually *teach* VERY well. What happened?
A. While *I was teaching, my supervisor was sitting at the back of the room and watching me.*
B. Oh. I bet that was a very difficult experience for you.
A. It was. *I was* very *nervous.*

Match

We often use colorful expressions to describe how we feel. Try to match the following expressions with the feelings they describe.

_____ 1. "My stomach is growling."   a. angry

_____ 2. "I can't keep my eyes open."   b. embarrassed

_____ 3. "I'm jumping for joy!"   c. bored

_____ 4. "I'm seeing red!"   d. nervous

_____ 5. "I'm ashamed to look at them straight in the eye."   e. scared

_____ 6. "I'm on pins and needles!"   f. hungry

_____ 7. "I'm shaking like a leaf!"   g. sad

_____ 8. "I'm feeling blue."   h. happy

IN YOUR OWN WORDS

For Writing and Discussion

A DIFFICULT EXPERIENCE

Tell about a difficult experience you had.

What happened?
How did you feel?

CHECK-UP

What's the Word?

I. Fill in the correct words and then practice the conversation.

A. _____₁ you sleep well last night?

B. No, I _____₂. I _____₃ too excited.

A. Oh? Why _____₄ you excited?

B. I _____₅ thinking about the job interview I had yesterday afternoon.

A. Oh? _____₆ you go to an interview yesterday?

B. Yes, I _____₇.

A. _____₈ you nervous?

B. No, I _____₉. The interviewer _____₁₀ very nice, and she _____₁₁ ask me any difficult questions.

A. _____₁₂ you get the job?

B. I _____₁₃ know yet. I'll find out today or tomorrow.

II. Choose the correct words to complete the questions and answers.

argue	bake	break	burn	cut	get
lose	meet	play	shop	slice	work

1. A. How did Ted _break_ his leg?
   B. He _broke_ it while _he_ _was_ _playing_ soccer.

2. A. How did Barbara _____ her purse?
   B. She _____ it while _____ _____ _____ at the supermarket after work today.

3. A. How did Jimmy _____ a bloody nose?
   B. He _____ it while _____ _____ _____ with the boy across the street.

4. A. How did Carol _____ the President?
   B. She _____ him while _____ _____ _____ in Washington.

5. A. How did Roger _____ his finger?
   B. He _____ it while _____ _____ _____ tomatoes.

6. A. How did you _____ yourself?
   B. I _____ myself while _____ _____ _____ cookies for my daughter and her friends.

Listening

Listen and choose the best answer.

1. a. Yes, I did.
   b. Yes, I was.

2. a. They cleaned their rooms.
   b. They were cleaning their rooms.

3. a. She played basketball.
   b. She was playing basketball.

4. a. He was nervous.
   b. He was looking over his shoulder.

5. a. I was bored.
   b. You were bored.

6. a. I was very hungry.
   b. I wasn't very hungry.

18

Tell Me About Your Vacation

1. Did you go to Paris?
   No, we didn't.
   Where did you go?
   We went to Rome.

2. Did you get there by boat?
   No, _____.
   How _____?
   _____ by plane.

3. Did your plane leave on time?
   No, _____.
   How late _____?
   _____ two hours late.

4. Did you have good weather during the flight?
   No, _____.
   What kind of _____?
   _____ terrible weather.

5. Did you stay in a big hotel?
   No, _____.
   What kind of _____?
   _____ a small hotel.

6. Did you eat in fancy restaurants?
   No, _____.
   Where _____?
   _____ cheap restaurants.

7. Did you speak Italian?
No, _____.
What language _____?
_____ English.

8. Did you take many pictures?
No, _____.
How many _____?
_____ just a few pictures.

9. Did you buy any clothing?
No, _____.
What _____?
_____ souvenirs.

10. Did you swim in the Mediterranean?
No, _____.
Where _____?
_____ in the pool at our hotel.

11. Did you see the Colosseum?
No, _____.
What _____?
_____ the Vatican.

12. Did you travel around the city by taxi?
No, _____.
How _____?
_____ by bus.

13. Did you send postcards to your
    friends?
    No, _____.
    Who _____?
    _____ our relatives.

14. Did you write to them about the
    monuments?
    No, _____.
    What _____?
    _____ the weather.

15. Did you meet a lot of Italians?
    No, _____.
    Who _____?
    _____ a lot of other tourists.

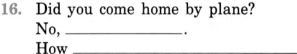

16. Did you come home by plane?
    No, _____.
    How _____?
    _____ by boat.

ON YOUR OWN: Trips and Travel

Did you take a trip this year? Did you travel to another city? Did you visit a friend or a relative out of town? Talk with other students in your class about your last trip:

Where did you go?
How did you get there?
Where did you stay?
What did you do there?
How long were you there?
Did you have a good time?

If you have some photographs of your last trip, bring them to class and talk about them with the other students.

GRAMMAR

Simple Past Tense

What did	I he she it we you they	do?		I He She It We You They	worked.	

Did	I he she it we you they	fall asleep?	Yes,	I he she it we you they	did.	No,	I he she it we you they	didn't.

I He She It	was			I He She It	wasn't	
We You They	were	tired.		We You They	weren't	tired.

Past Continuous Tense

I He She It	was	
We You They	were	working.

Irregular Verbs
break–broke
buy–bought
come–came
cut–cut
eat–ate
get–got
go–went
have–had
hurt–hurt
leave–left
lose–lost
meet–met
ride–rode
see–saw
send–sent
sing–sang
speak–spoke
swim–swam
take–took
teach–taught
write–wrote

FUNCTIONS

Asking for and Reporting Information

Who *did you send postcards to*?

What did you *buy*?
What did *he* do yesterday?
What were you doing?
What happened?
What language *did you speak*?
What kind of *weather did you have*?

Where were you?
Where did you go?

Why?

How did *John break his arm*?
How did you feel?
How did you get there?
How did you meet *your husband*?
How many *pictures did you take*?
How long were you there?
How late did *your plane leave*?

Did *Sam do well on his exam*?
  Yes, *he* did.
  No, *he* didn't.
Did you have a good time?

Admitting Poor Performance

I didn't *teach* very well *this morning*.
I *taught* very badly.

Indicating Lack of Understanding

I don't understand.

Initiating a Topic

You know . . .

Making a Deduction

I bet *that was a difficult experience for you.*

Review:
  Future: Going to ■
  Future: Will ■
  Future Continuous Tense ■
  Time Expressions ■
  Possessive Pronouns ■

What Are They Going to Do?

(I am)	I'm	
(He is)	He's	
(She is)	She's	going to read.
(It is)	It's	
(We are)	We're	
(You are)	You're	
(They are)	They're	

	am	I	
What is		he / she / it	going to do?
	are	we / you / they	

Time Expressions

yesterday
this   } morning, afternoon, evening
tomorrow

last night
tonight
tomorrow night

last } week, month, year, Sunday, Monday,...
this } spring, summer,...
next } January, February,...

A. Are you going to plant carrots this year?

B. No, I'm not. I planted carrots LAST year.

A. What are you going to plant?

B. I'm going to plant tomatoes.

1. Is Ted going to wear his blue suit today?

   his black suit

2. Is Barbara going to cook fish tonight?

   chicken

3. Are you and your family going to Europe this summer?

   Mexico

4. Is Charlie going to play popular music this evening?

   jazz

5. Are you going to give your brother a watch for his birthday this year?

   a tie

6. Are Mr. and Mrs. Peterson going to watch the football game on Channel 2 this Monday night?

   the movie on Channel 4

7. Is Professor Hawkins going to teach European History this semester?

   Latin American History

8. Are you going to take ballet lessons this year?

   tap dance lessons

9. Is Mrs. McCarthy going to buy grapes this week?

   bananas

10. Are you going to call the landlord this time?

    the plumber

READING

PLANS FOR THE WEEKEND

It's Friday afternoon, and all the employees at the Acme Insurance Company are thinking about their plans for the weekend. Doris is going to plant flowers in her yard. Michael is going to paint his house. Tom and Jane are going to go to the beach. Peter is going to play baseball with his children. Rita is going to go camping in the mountains. And Karen and her friends are going to have a picnic.

Unfortunately, the employees at the Acme Insurance Company are going to be very disappointed. According to the radio, it's going to rain cats and dogs all weekend.

 CHECK-UP

Q & A

The employees of the Acme Insurance Company are talking with each other. Using this model, create dialogs based on the story.

A. Tell me, *Doris,* what are you going to do this weekend?
B. I'm going to *plant flowers in my yard.* How about YOU, *Michael?* What are YOU going to do?
A. I'm going to *paint my house.*
B. Well, have a nice weekend.
A. You, too.

What are you going to do this weekend?
What's the weather forecast?

Listening

Listen to the conversation and choose the answer that is true.

1. a. He's going to wear his blue suit.
   b. He's going to wear his black suit.

2. a. He's going to make spaghetti and meatballs for dinner.
   b. He's going to make beef stew for dinner.

3. a. They're going to go to the movies.
   b. They're going to watch TV.

4. a. He's going to go to the supermarket tomorrow.
   b. He's going to work in his garden tomorrow.

5. a. He's going to call a mechanic.
   b. He's going to call a plumber.

6. a. They're going to buy the car.
   b. They aren't going to buy the car.

Will Richard Get Out of the Hospital Soon?

(I will)	I'll	
(He will)	He'll	
(She will)	She'll	
(It will)	It'll	work.
(We will)	We'll	
(You will)	You'll	
(They will)	They'll	

I	
He	
She	
It	won't work.
We	(will not)
You	
They	

A. Will Richard get out of the hospital soon?

B. Yes, he will. He'll get out in a few days.

A. Will Sherman get out of the hospital soon?

B. No, he won't. He won't get out for a few weeks.

1. Will the movie begin soon?
   Yes, _____. _____ at 8:00.

2. Will the game begin soon?
   No, _____. _____ until 3:00.

3. Will Bob and Betty see each other again soon?
   Yes, ____. ____ this Saturday night.

4. Will John and Julia see each other again soon?
   No, _____. _____ until next year.

5. Will the soup be ready soon?
   Yes, _____. _____ in a few minutes.

6. Will the turkey be ready soon?
   No, _____. _____ for several hours.

7. Will Mom be back soon?
   Yes, _____. _____ in a little while.

8. Will Shirley be back soon?
   No, _____. _____ for a long time.

Will You Be Home This Evening?

I'll
He'll
She'll
It'll
We'll
You'll
They'll
} be working.

A. Will you be home this evening?

B. Yes, I will. I'll be **watching** TV.

A. Will Jane be home this evening?

B. No, she won't. She'll be **working late at the office**.

1. Tom
   read

2. Mr. and Mrs. Harris
   paint their bathroom

3. you
   swim

4. Sheila
   do her laundry

5. you and your family
   ice skate

6. Sally
   clean her apartment

7. Mr. and Mrs. Grant
   shop

8. Donald
   fill out his income tax
   form

9. you
   visit a friend in the
   hospital

Can You Call Back a Little Later?

Hi, _____. This is _____. Can you talk for a minute?

I'm sorry. I can't talk right now. I'm _____ing. Can you call back a little later?

Sure. How much longer will you be _____ing?

I'll probably be _____ing for another _____ minutes.

Fine. I'll call you in _____ minutes.

Speak to you soon.

Good-bye.

Create conversations based on the model above.

1. *study English*

2. *help my children with their homework*

3. *wash my kitchen floor*

4. *have dinner with my family*

5. *give the kids a bath*

6.

SAYING GOOD-BYE

Mr. and Mrs. Anastas are at the Athens Airport. They're saying good-bye to their son Dimitri and his family. It's a very emotional day. In a few minutes, Dimitri and his family will get on a plane and fly to the United States. They won't be coming back. They're leaving Greece permanently, and Mr. and Mrs. Anastas won't be seeing them for a long, long time.

Dimitri and his family are going to live in Chicago. They're going to stay with his wife's relatives. Dimitri will work in the family's restaurant. His wife, Anna, will take any job she can find during the day, and she'll study English at night. The children will begin school in September.

Mr. and Mrs. Anastas are both happy and sad. They're happy because they know their son and his family will have a good life in their new home. However, they're sad because they know they're going to be very lonely. Their house will be quiet and empty, they'll have to celebrate holidays by themselves, and they won't see their grandchildren grow up.

Some day Mr. and Mrs. Anastas will visit Chicago, or perhaps they'll even move there. But until then, they're going to miss their family very much. As you can imagine, it's very difficult for them to say good-bye.

IN YOUR OWN WORDS

✔CHECK-UP

True or False?

1. Dimitri and his family will be leaving Greece for a few minutes.
2. Anna's relatives live in Chicago.
3. Mr. Anastas is happy and Mrs. Anastas is sad.
4. Mr. and Mrs. Anastas might move to Chicago.
5. Mr. and Mrs. Anastas are sad because they'll be at the Athens Airport until they visit Chicago or move there.

For Writing and Discussion

1. **Tell about an emotional day in your life when you had to say good-bye.**

2. **Tell about your plans for the future.**

   How long are you going to study English?
   What are you going to do after you finish?
   What kind of work are you going to do?
   Where are you going to live?

Could You Possibly Do Me a Favor?

I	me	mine
he	him	his
she	her	hers
it	it	its
we	us	ours
you	you	yours
they	them	theirs

A. Could you possibly do me a favor?*

B. Sure. What is it?

A. I've got a problem. I have to fix my roof and I don't have a ladder. Could I possibly borrow YOURS?

B. I'm sorry. I'm afraid I don't have one.

A. Oh. Do you know anybody who DOES?

B. Yes. You should call Charlie. I'm sure he'll be happy to lend you his.

A. Thank you. I'll call him right away.

*Or: Could you do a favor for me? Could I ask you a favor?

A. Could you possibly do me a favor?*

B. Sure. What is it?

A. I've got a problem. I have to _____ and I don't have a _____. Could I possibly borrow YOURS?

B. I'm sorry. I'm afraid I don't have one.

A. Oh. Do you know anybody who DOES?

B. Yes. You should call _____. I'm sure _____'ll be happy to lend you _____ (his, hers, theirs).

A. Thank you. I'll call _____ (him, her, them) right away.

*Or: Could you do a favor for me? Could I ask you a favor?

1. *fix my TV set*
   screwdriver

2. *fix my front door*
   hammer

3. *write a composition for my English class*
   dictionary

4. *fix my flat tire*
   jack

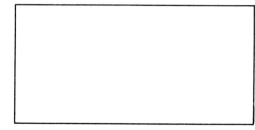

5. *go to a wedding*
   tuxedo

6.

1. John is looking forward to this weekend. He isn't going to think about work. He's going to read a few magazines, fix his car, and relax at home with his family.

2. Alice is looking forward to her birthday. Her sister is going to have a party for her, and all her friends are going to be there.

3. Mr. and Mrs. Williams are looking forward to their summer vacation. They're going to go camping in the mountains. They're going to hike several miles every day, take a lot of pictures, and forget about all their problems at home.

4. George is looking forward to his retirement. He's going to get up late every morning, visit friends every afternoon, and enjoy quiet evenings at home with his wife.

What are YOU looking forward to? A birthday? A holiday? A day off? Talk about it with other students in your class.

What are you looking forward to?
When is it going to happen?
What are you going to do?

GRAMMAR

Future: Going to

What	am	I	going to do?
	is	he she it	
	are	we you they	

(I am)	I'm	going to read.
(He is)	He's	
(She is)	She's	
(It is)	It's	
(We are)	We're	
(You are)	You're	
(They are)	They're	

Possessive Pronouns

mine
his
hers
its
ours
yours
theirs

Future: Will

(I will)	I'll	work.
(He will)	He'll	
(She will)	She'll	
(It will)	It'll	
(We will)	We'll	
(You will)	You'll	
(They will)	They'll	

I He She It We You They	won't work.

Future Continuous Tense

(I will)	I'll	be working.
(He will)	He'll	
(She will)	She'll	
(It will)	It'll	
(We will)	We'll	
(You will)	You'll	
(They will)	They'll	

FUNCTIONS

Asking for and Reporting Information

Will *Richard get out of the hospital soon?*
Yes, *he* will.
No, *he* won't.

Will you *be home this evening?*
Yes, I will. I'll be *watching TV.*
No, I won't. I'll be *working late at the office.*

Will *the movie* begin soon?
Will *the soup* be ready soon?
Will *Mom* be back soon?

How much longer will you be *studying English?*
I'll probably be *studying English* for another *30* minutes.

What are you looking forward to?
When is it going to happen?

What's the weather forecast?

Do you know anybody who *has a ladder?*

Tell me, *Doris,* _____?

Inquiring about Intention

What are you going to do?
What are you going to do *this weekend?*
What are you going to *plant?*

Are you going to *plant carrots this year?*

Expressing Intention

I'm going to *plant tomatoes.*

I'll *call you in 30 minutes.*
I'll *call him right away.*

Expressing Probability

I'll probably be *studying English for another 30 minutes.*

Requesting

Could you possibly do me a favor?
Could you do a favor for me?
Could I ask you a favor?

Could I possibly *borrow yours?*

Responding to Requests

Sure. What is it?

Greeting People

Hi, _____. This is _____.

Can you talk for a minute?
I'm sorry. I can't talk right now.
I'm *studying English.* Can you call back a little later?

Leave Taking

Well, have a nice weekend.
You, too.

Speak to you soon.
Good-bye.

Apologizing

I'm sorry.

Expressing Inability

I'm sorry. I can't *talk right now.*

Expressing Obligation

I have to *fix my roof.*

Admitting

I'm afraid *I don't have one.*

Offering Advice

You should *call Charlie.*

Expressing Certainty

I'm sure *he'll be happy to lend you his.*

Expressing Gratitude

Thank you.

Present Perfect Tense ■

They've Already Seen a Movie This Week

(I have)	I've
(We have)	We've
(You have)	You've
(They have)	They've } eaten.
(He has)	He's
(She has)	She's
(It has)	It's

A. Are Mr. and Mrs. Smith going to **see** a movie tonight?

B. No, they aren't. They've already **seen** a movie this week.

A. Really? When?

B. They **saw** a movie yesterday.

1. Are Mr. and Mrs. Smith going to eat at a restaurant tonight?

   eat–ate–eaten

2. Is Frank going to get a haircut today?

   get–got–gotten

3. Is Lucy going to write to her best friend today?

   write–wrote–written

4. Is Bob going to take his children to the zoo today?

   take–took–taken

5. Are you going to give blood today?
give–gave–given

6. Are you and your friends going to see a play this evening?
see–saw–seen

7. Is Jennifer going to go to a concert tonight?
go–went–gone

8. Is Philip going to wear his red tie today?
wear–wore–worn

9. Is Mary going to do her food shopping today?
do–did–done

10. Is Max going to swim at the health club today?
swim–swam–swum

11. Is Marion going to wash her car today?
wash–washed–washed

12. Is Clara going to play Bingo today?
play–played–played

13. Are you going to buy bananas today?
buy–bought–bought

14. Is Tom going to spend a lot of money at the department store today?
spend–spent–spent

READING

WE CAN'T DECIDE

My friends and I can't decide what to do tonight. I don't want to see a movie. I've already seen a movie this week. Jack doesn't want to go bowling. He has already gone bowling this week. Nancy doesn't want to eat at a restaurant. She has already eaten at a restaurant this week. Betsy and Philip don't want to play cards. They have already played cards this week. And NOBODY wants to go dancing. We have all gone dancing this week.

It's already 9 P.M., and we still haven't decided what we're going to do tonight.

✓ CHECK-UP

Group Conversation

You and other students in your class are the people in this story. In a small group, create a group conversation. Use the lines below to get your conversation started.

A. Look! It's already 9 P.M., and we still haven't decided what we're going to do tonight. Does anybody have any ideas?
B. I don't know.
C. Do you want to see a movie?
D. No, not me. I've already . . .
E. Does anybody want to . . . ?
F. I don't. I've already . . .
G. I have an idea. Let's . . .
H. No, I don't want to do that. I've already . . .

.
.
.

What's the Word?

Fill in the correct words to complete the story.

Alvin has a very bad cold. He has felt* miserable all week, and he still feels miserable now. He's very upset. He has tried very hard to get rid of his cold, but nothing he has done has helped. At the beginning of the week, he went to a clinic and saw a doctor. He followed the doctor's advice all week. He stayed home, took aspirin, drank† orange juice, ate chicken soup, and rested in bed.

At this point, Alvin is extremely frustrated. Even though he has _gone_ to a clinic and _saw_ a doctor, _stayed_ home, _took_ aspirin, _drank_ orange juice, _ate_ chicken soup, and _rested_ in bed, he STILL has a very bad cold. Nothing he has _done_ has helped.

We hope you feel better soon, Alvin!

*feel–felt–felt
†drink–drank–drunk

38

They Just Haven't Had the Time

I We You They	} haven't (have not)	
He She It	} hasn't (has not)	eaten.*

swam

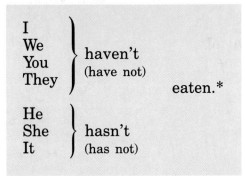

A. Do you like to swim?

B. Yes, I do. But I haven't swum in a long time.

A. Why not?

B. I just haven't had the time.

1. Does Kathy like to (go) camping?

2. Does Robert like to (do) his English homework?

3. Do you like to (read) the *New York Times*?

4. Do you and your sister like to (play) Monopoly?

5. Do Bob and Sally like to (take) dance lessons?

6. Does Betsy like to (make) her own clothes?

7. Does William like to (write) poetry?

8. Do you like to see your old friends?

9.

*In the present perfect tense the word after **have** or **has** is a past participle. Some past participles (**read, baked, made**) are the same as the past tense. Other past participles (**swum, gone, done**) are different from the past tense. We will tell you when the past participles are different. A list of these words is in the Appendix at the end of the book.

Have You Seen the New Walt Disney Movie Yet?

Have	{ I / we / you / they }	eaten?	Yes,	{ I / we / you / they }	have.
Has	{ he / she / it }			{ he / she / it }	has.

A. Have you **seen** the new Walt Disney movie yet?

B. Yes, I have. I **saw** it yesterday.

1. *you* written
   write your composition ¾
   wrote

2. *Nancy* ridden
   ride her new bicycle*
   rode

3. *Arthur* taken
   take his driver's test
   took

4. *Sharon and Charles* done
   do their homework
   did

5. *you* read
   read Chapter 3 ¾ to

6. *David* gotten
   get his paycheck
   got

7. *Mr. and Mrs. Chang* made
   make plans for the
   weekend
   made

8. *Stanley* worn
   wear his new suit
   wore

9. *you* met
   meet your new
   English teacher
   met

*ride–rode–ridden

40

Has Peter Left for Work Yet?

Have	I we you they	eaten?	No,	I we you they	haven't.
Has	he she it			he she it	hasn't.

A. Has Peter left for work yet? とこ す

B. No, he hasn't. He has to leave now.

1. *Mildred*
taken
take her medicine

2. *you*
finished
finish your homework

3. *Bill*
gotten
get up

4. *John and Julia*
said
say good-bye

5. *you*
fed
feed the dog

6. *Barbara*
called
call her boss

7. *Timmy*
gone
go to bed

8. *you*
spoken my
*speak to your landlord** ろ が
iot

9. *Harry*
paid   i ﾟﾞﾞ electric
pay his electric bill

*speak–spoke–spoken

41

WORKING OVERTIME

I'm an employee of the Goodwell Computer Company. This is a typical Friday afternoon at our office. All the employees are working overtime. We haven't gone home because we haven't finished our work yet. Friday is always a very busy day.

The secretary still hasn't typed two important letters. The bookkeeper hasn't written all the paychecks. The office clerks haven't delivered all the mail. And the boss still hasn't spoken to three important people who are waiting to see him.

As for me, I'm the custodian, and I haven't finished my work yet either. I still haven't cleaned all the offices because my co-workers haven't gone home yet! I'm not really surprised. Friday is always a very busy day at our office.

 *CHECK-UP*

Q & A

The custodian at the Goodwell Computer Company is talking with the employees on a typical Friday afternoon. Using this model, create dialogs based on the story.

A. I see you haven't gone home yet.
B. No, I haven't. I still haven't *typed two important letters*.
A. Well, have a good weekend.
B. You, too.

What's the Word?

1. A. Have you (see) _Seen_ the letter from the Acme Company?
   B. Yes. I _saw_ it on your desk.

2. A. Have you (eat) _eaten_ lunch yet?
   B. Yes. I _ate_ a few minutes ago.

3. A. Has the bookkeeper (go) _gone_ to the bank yet?
   B. Yes, she _has_. She _went_ there this morning.

4. A. Have you (speak) _spoken_ to the boss about your vacation?
   B. Yes, I _have_. I _spoke_ to her about it yesterday.

5. A. Have you (make) _made_ plans for my trip to Chicago yet?
   B. Yes. I _made_ them yesterday.

6. A. Has anybody (read) _read_ today's *New York Times*?
   B. Yes. I _read_ it on my way to work.

7. A. Has the office clerk (take) _taken_ the mail to the post office yet?
   B. No, he _hasn't_. He _took_ it to the mail room ten minutes ago, but _he_ _hasn't_ _taken_ it to the post office yet.

8. A. Has John (finish) _finished_ his work for the day?
   B. Yes, he _has_. He's already (go) _gone_ home.

Have You Seen Any Good Movies Recently?

A. What are you going to do tonight?

B. I'm not sure. I really want to see a good movie. I haven't seen a good movie in a long time.

A. What movie are you going to see?

B. I don't know. Have you seen any good movies recently?

A. Yes, I have. I saw a VERY good movie just last week.

B. Really? What movie did you see?

A. I saw *The Return of Superman*.

B. And you liked it?

A. I LOVED it! I think it's one of the BEST movies I've ever seen.

A. What are you going to do tonight? *go to* *night club*

B. I'm not sure. I really want to _eat at_ a good _restaurant_.
I haven't _eaten at_ *(gone to)* a good _restaurant_ *(night club)* in a long time.

A. What _restaurant_ *(night club)* are you going to _eat at_ *(go)*?

B. I don't know. *san yü* Have you _eaten at_ *(gone to)* any good _restaurant_s *(night club)*
recently? *zuì jìn*

A. Yes, I have. I _ate at_ *(went to)* a VERY good _restaurant_ *(night club)* just last week.

B. Really? What _restaurant_ *(night club)* did you _eat at_ *(go)*?

A. I _ate at_ *(went to)* "*the* _chinese restaurant_."

B. And you liked it?

A. I LOVED it! I think it's one of the BEST _restaurant_s *(night club)* I've ever *céng jìng*
eaten *(gone)*.

1. *read – book*
fax
non–fiction

2. *eat at – restaurant*

3. *see – play*
Seen

44

Saw *romàntic 浪漫的*

4. *go to – night club 夜总会*
KlAb
gone
went

READING

SHARON LIKES NEW YORK

Sharon has lived in New York for a long time. She has done a lot of things in New York. She has seen several plays, she has gone to the top of the Empire State Building, she has visited the Statue of Liberty, and she has taken a tour of the United Nations.

However, there's a lot she hasn't done yet. She hasn't gone to a concert, she hasn't spent time at any art museums, and she hasn't gone to the top of the World Trade Center.

Sharon likes New York. She has done a lot of things, and there's still a lot more to do.

✔ CHECK-UP

Listening

Sharon is on vacation in San Francisco. She's checking her list of things to do while she's on vacation. On the list below, check the things Sharon has already done.

- —— see the Golden Gate Bridge
- —— visit Golden Gate Park
- —— take a tour of Alcatraz Prison
- —✗ go to Chinatown
- —— eat at Fisherman's Wharf
- —— buy souvenirs

Alan is a secretary in a very busy office. He's checking his list of things to do before 5 P.M. on Friday. On the list below, check the things Alan has already done.

- —— call Mrs. Porter
- —— type the letter to the Ajax Insurance Company
- —— go to the bank
- —— take the mail to the post office
- —— clean the coffee machine
- —— speak to the boss about my salary

It's Saturday, and Judy and Paul Johnson are doing lots of things around the house. They're checking the list of things they have to do today. On the list below, check the things they've already done.

- —— do the laundry   *yet*
- —— wash the kitchen windows
- —— pay the bills
- —— clean the garage
- —— fix the bathroom sink
- —— vacuum the living room

✏ IN YOUR OWN WORDS

For Writing and Discussion

1. Tell about your experiences in the place where you live.
   What have you done? What haven't you done yet?

2. Make a list of things you usually do at school, at work, or at home. Check the things you've already done this week. Share your list with other students in your class. Tell about what you've done and what you haven't done.

45

CHAPTER 4 SUMMARY

Grammar

Present Perfect Tense

(I have)	I've	
(We have)	We've	
(You have)	You've	
(They have)	They've	eaten.
(He has)	He's	
(She has)	She's	
(It has)	It's	

I We You They	haven't	
He She It	hasn't	eaten.

Have	I we you they	eaten?
Has	he she it	

Yes,	I we you they	have.
	he she it	has.

No,	I we you they	haven't.
	he she it	hasn't.

Irregular Verbs

do – did – done	see – saw – seen
drink – drank – drunk	speak – spoke – spoken
eat – ate – eaten	swim – swam – swum
get – got – gotten	take – took – taken
give – gave – given	wear – wore – worn
go – went – gone	write – wrote – written
ride – rode – ridden	

buy – bought – bought	read – read – read
feed – fed – fed	say – said – said
feel – felt – felt	spend – spent – spent
leave – left – left	
make – made – made	
meet – met – met	
pay – paid – paid	

FUNCTIONS

Asking for and Reporting Information

I've already *given blood this week.*
  Really? When?
I *gave blood yesterday.*

I haven't *swum* in a long time.
  Why not?
I just haven't had the time.

Have you *seen the new Walt Disney movie* yet?
  Yes, I have. I *saw it yesterday.*

Has *Peter left for work* yet?
  No, *he* hasn't.

I still haven't *typed two important letters.*

Have you *seen any good movies* recently?
  Yes, I have. I *saw a very good movie just last week.*
What *movie* did you *see?*
  I *saw The Return of Superman.*

Inquiring about Intention

Are you going to *give blood today?*

What are you going to do *tonight?*

What *movie* are you going to *see?*

Expressing Uncertainty

I'm not sure.

I don't know.

Expressing Want-Desire

I really want to *see a good movie.*

Inquiring about Likes/Dislikes

Do you like to *swim?*

And you liked it?

Expressing Likes

I LOVED it!

Expressing Obligation

I have to *finish it now.*
He has to *leave now.*

Expressing an Opinion

I think *it's* one of the best *movies* I've ever *seen.*

Initiating a Conversation

I see *you haven't gone home yet.*

Expressing Agreement

That's right.

Leave Taking

Have a good weekend.
  You, too.

Present Perfect vs. Present Tense ■
Present Perfect vs. Past Tense ■
Since/For ■

How Long?

for	since
three hours	three o'clock
two days	yesterday afternoon
a week	last week
a long time	1960
•	•
•	•
•	•

A. How long have you known* each other?

B. We've known each other **for two years.**

A. How long have you been† sick?

B. I've been sick **since last Thursday.**

1. How long have Don and Patty known each other?

for three years

2. How long have Mr. and Mrs. Peterson been married?

Since 1945

*know–knew–known
†be–was–been

3. How long has Tommy liked girls?
He's
Since *last year*

4. How long have you had a headache?
I've
Since *ten o'clock this morning*

5. How long has Diane had the measles?
She's
for *five days*

6. How long has Mrs. Brown been a teacher?
She's
for *thirteen years*

7. How long have there been satellites in space?
have ... been
Since *1957*

8. How long have you owned this car?
I've
for *five and a half years*

9. How long has John owned his own house?
He's
Since *1981*

10. How long have you been interested in astronomy?
I've
for *many years*

11. How long has Lucy been interested in computer technology?
She's
for *a long time*

12. How long have you been here? Since 1994
I've
1963

49

A VERY DEDICATED DOCTOR

Dr. Fernando's waiting room is very full today. A lot of people are waiting to see him, and they're hoping that the doctor can help them. George's neck has been stiff for more than a week. Martha has had a bad headache since yesterday, and Lenny has felt dizzy since early this morning. Carol has had a high fever for two days, Bob's knee has been swollen for three weeks, Bill's arm has been black and blue since last weekend, and Tommy and Julie have had little red spots all over their bodies for the past twenty-four hours.

Dr. Fernando has been in the office since early this morning. He has already seen a lot of patients, and he will certainly see many more before the day is over. Dr. Fernando's patients don't know it, but he also isn't feeling well. He has had a pain in his back since last Thursday, but he hasn't taken any time to stay at home and rest. He has had a lot of patients this week, and he's a very dedicated doctor.

Q & A

Dr. Fernando's patients are talking to him about their problems. Using this model, create dialogs based on the story.

A. So how are you feeling today, *George?*
B. Not very well, Dr. Fernando.
A. What seems to be the problem?
B. *My neck is stiff.*
A. I see. Tell me, how long *has your neck been stiff?*
B. *For more than a week.*

Choose

1. They've known each other since
   a. 1985.
   b. three years.

2. I've been interested in history for
   a. last year.
   b. one year.

3. She has been a doctor for
   a. two years ago.
   b. two years.

4. I've had a backache since
   a. yesterday.
   b. two days.

5. We've been here for
   a. one hour.
   b. one o'clock.

6. There have been two robberies in our neighborhood since
   a. one month.
   b. last month.

7. My grandparents have owned this house for
   a. a long time.
   b. many years ago.

8. They've been in love since
   a. last spring.
   b. three months.

Choose

1. My right arm has been very
   a. dizzy.
   b. stiff.

2. My son has a high
   a. fever.
   b. pain.

3. How long has your arm been
   a. nauseous?
   b. swollen?

4. Jeff's leg has been black and
   a. blue.
   b. red.

5. I've looked at your X-rays, and I think you have
   a. lungs.
   b. pneumonia.

6. Look! I have spots all over my
   a. measles!
   b. body!

Since I Was a Little Boy

A. Do you know Mrs. Potter?

B. Yes, I do. I've known her for a long time.

A. Oh, really? That's interesting. Tell me, how long have you known her?

B. I've known her **since I was a little boy.**

A. Are you two engaged?

B. Yes, we are. We've been engaged for a long time.

A. Oh, really? That's interesting. Tell me, how long have you been engaged?

B. We've been engaged **since we finished high school.**

1. Does your brother play the piano?
since he was eight years old

2. Is your friend Victor a professional musician?
since he finished college

3. **Do you have a personal computer?**
since I started college

4. **Are you interested in modern art?**
since I read about Picasso

5. **Is Jeffrey interested in French history?**
since he visited Paris

6. **Do you like jazz?**
since I was a teenager

7. **Do you know how to ski?**
since we were very young

8. **Does Johnny know how to count to ten?**
since he was two years old

9. **Do you own your own business?**
since I got out of the army

10. **Do you want to be an actress?**
since I saw "The Sound of Music"

11. **Do you have termites?**
since we bought the house

12. **Do your children know about "the birds and the bees"?***
since they were nine years old

*The facts of life.

Has Ralph Always Been a Carpenter?

A. Has Ralph always been a carpenter?

B. No. **He's been** a carpenter for the last ten years. Before that, **he was** a painter.

A. Have you always taught history?

B. No. **I've taught** history since 1980. Before that, **I taught** geography. 地理学

1. Has Fred always been thin?
the last three years
An American political scandal in 1973–74.

3. Have you always liked classical music? 古典的
the past few years

2. Has Roberta always had short hair?
she finished college

4. Have your parents always been Democrats? 民主主义者
Watergate* 水门事件

5. Has Steven always spoken with a
Boston accent? 口音

Since **he moved to Boston** *Before that.*
he spoken a New York accent

7. Has Andy always wanted to be an
astronaut? 太空人

Since **last September** *Before that.*
he wanted to be a policeman

9. Has Janet always known all the
people in her apartment building?

Since **the fire last year** *Before that.*
She knew just a few people

6. Have you always had a dog? *for*
the past five or six years *Before that*
I had a cat.

8. Has Louis always been the store
manager?

for **the last six months** *Before that*
he was a cashier.

10. Has Larry always owned a
sports car?

Since **he won the lottery** 彩券 *Before that*
he owned a bicycle.

Answer these questions and then ask other students in your class.

1. What is your present address?
   How long have you lived there?
2. What was your last address?
   How long did you live there?

3. Who is the President/Prime Minister of your country?
   How long has he/she been the President/Prime Minister?
4. Who was the last President/Prime Minister of your country?
   How long was he/she the President/Prime Minister?

5. Who is your English teacher now?
   How long has he/she been your English teacher?
6. Who was your last English teacher?
   How long was he/she your English teacher?

READING

A WONDERFUL FAMILY

Mr. and Mrs. Patterson are very proud of their family. Their daughter, Ruth, is a very successful engineer. She has been an engineer since she finished college. Her husband's name is Pablo. They have been happily married for thirty-five years. Pablo is a professional guitarist. He has known how to play the guitar since he was four years old.

Ruth and Pablo have two children. Their son, David, is a computer programmer. He has been interested in computers since he was a teenager. Their daughter, Rita, is a doctor. She has been a doctor since she finished medical school in 1981.

Mr. and Mrs. Patterson also have a son, Herbert. Herbert is single. He has been a bachelor all his life. He's a famous journalist. They haven't seen him since he moved to Singapore several years ago.

Mr. and Mrs. Patterson feel fortunate to have such wonderful children and grandchildren. They're very proud of them.

 CHECK-UP

True or False?

1. Ruth's husband is a professional violinist.
2. Ruth and Pablo have two teenagers.
3. The Pattersons' grandson is interested in computers.
4. Rita has been in medical school since 1981.
5. Herbert has never been married.
6. Herbert hasn't seen his parents since they moved to Singapore several years ago.

Listening

Listen to the conversation and choose the answer that is true.

1. a. He doesn't have a toothache now.
   b. He still has a toothache.

2. a. His knee isn't swollen now.
   b. His knee is still swollen.

3. a. Her father is an engineer.
   b. Her father isn't an engineer.

4. a. She's a teenager.
   b. She isn't a teenager.

5. a. He has lived in Rome for 5 years.
   b. He lived in Rome for 5 years.

6. a. Jim has lived in Greece.
   b. Jim lives in Greece.

7. a. Betty went home 2 days ago.
   b. Betty hasn't been home for 2 days.

8. a. He has lived in Nashville for 7 years.
   b. He lived in Nashville for 7 years.

WORKING THEIR WAY UP TO THE TOP

Louis is very successful. For the past six years, he has been the manager of the Big Value Supermarket on Grant Street. Louis has worked very hard to get where he is today. First, he was a clerk for two years. Then, he was a cashier for three years. After that, he was an assistant manager for five years. Finally, six years ago, he became the manager of the store. Everybody at the Big Value Supermarket is very proud of Louis. He started at the bottom, and he has worked his way up to the top.

Florence is very successful. For the past two years, she has been the president of the Jason Department Store Corporation. Florence has worked very hard to get where she is today. She started her career at the Jason Department Store in Nashville, Tennessee. First, she was a salesperson in the Children's Clothing Department for three years. Then, she was the manager of the Women's Clothing Department for ten years. Then, she was the store manager for eight years. After that, she moved to New York and became a vice-president of the corporation. Finally, two years ago, she became the president. Everybody at the Jason Department Store in Nashville is very proud of Florence. She started at the bottom, and she has worked her way up to the top.

✔ CHECK-UP

True, False, or Maybe?

Answer True, False, or Maybe (if the answer isn't in the story).

1. Louis started as a cashier at the Big Value Supermarket.
2. He has worked there for sixteen years.
3. All employees at the Big Value Supermarket start at the bottom.
4. Florence has been the manager of the Women's Clothing Department in Nashville for ten years.
5. The Children's Clothing Department was on the bottom floor of the store.
6. Florence hasn't been a vice-president for two years.

✏ IN YOUR OWN WORDS

For Writing and Discussion

Tell a story about your English teacher.

How long have you know him/her?
How long has he/she been an English teacher?
What did he/she do before that? How long?
Where does he/she live?
How long has he/she lived there?
Has he/she lived anywhere else? Where? How long?
Is he/she married? How long?
Besides teaching English, what is your English teacher interested in?
How long has he/she been interested in that?

A. George!

B. Tony! I can't believe it's you! I haven't seen you in years.

A. That's right, George. It's been a long time. How have you been?

B. Fine. And how about YOU?

A. Everything's fine with me, too.

B. Tell me, Tony, do you still live on Main Street?

A. No. I haven't lived on Main Street for several years.

B. Where do you live NOW?

A. I live on River Road. And how about YOU? Do you still live on Central Avenue?

B. No. I haven't lived on Central Avenue since 1975.

A. Where do you live NOW?

B. I live on Park Boulevard.

A. Tell me, George, are you still a barber?

B. No. I haven't been a barber for several years.

A. Really? What do you do NOW?

B. I'm a taxi driver. And how about YOU? Are you still a painter?

A. No. I haven't been a painter for a long time.

B. Really? What do you do NOW?

A. I'm a carpenter.

B. Tell me, Tony, do you still play the saxophone?

A. No. I haven't played the saxophone for many years. And how about YOU? Do you still go fishing on Saturday mornings?

B. No. I haven't gone fishing on Saturday mornings since I got married.

A. Well, George, I'm afraid I have to go now. We should get together soon.

B. Good idea, Tony. It's been a long time.

Pretend that it's ten years from now. You're walking along the street and suddenly you meet a student who was in your English class. Try this conversation. Remember, you haven't seen this person for ten years.

A. _George_!

B. _Tony_! I can't believe it's you! I haven't seen you in years.

A. That's right, _George_. It's been a long time. How have you been?

B. Fine. And how about YOU?

A. Everything's fine with me, too.

B. Tell me, _Tony_, do you still live on _Main Street_?

A. No. I haven't lived on _Main Street_ (for/since) _several years_.

B. Where do you live NOW?

A. I live on _River Road_. And how about YOU? Do you still live on _Central Avenue_?

B. No. I haven't lived on _Central Avenue_ (for/since) _1975_.

A. Where do you live NOW?

B. I live on _Park Boulevard_.

A. Tell me, _George_, are you still a _barber_?

B. No. I haven't been a _barber_ (for/since) _several years_.

A. Really? What do you do NOW?

B. I'm a _taxi driver_. And how about YOU? Are you still a _painter_?

A. No. I haven't been a _painter_ (for/since) _a long time_.

B. Really? What do you do NOW?

A. I'm a _carpenter_.

B. Tell me, _Tony_, do you still _play the_ _saxophone_?

A. No. I haven't _played_ (for/since) _many years_. And how about YOU? Do you still _go fishing_?

B. No. I haven't _gone fishing_ (for/since) _I got married_.

A. Well, _George_, I'm afraid I have to go now. We should get together soon.

B. Good idea, _Tony_. It's been a long time.

CHAPTER 5 *SUMMARY*

Grammar

Since/For

We've known each other	since	three o'clock. yesterday afternoon. last week. 1960. we were in high school.
	for	three hours. two days. a week. a long time.

Irregular Verbs

be– was –been
know–knew–known

Present Perfect vs. Present Tense

I know Mrs. Potter.
I've known her since I was a little boy.

Present Perfect vs. Past Tense

Ralph was a painter.
He**'s been** a carpenter for the last ten years.

FUNCTIONS

Asking for and Reporting Information

How long *has your neck been stiff*?
  For *more than a week*.

Do you know *Mrs. Potter*?
  Yes, I do. I've known *her* for a long time.

How long have you *known each other*?
  We've known each other for *two years*.
  We've known each other since *1960*.

Has *Ralph* always been *a carpenter*?
  No. *He's been* a carpenter *for the last ten years*.
  Before that, *he was* a painter.

Have *you* always *taught history*?
  No. *I've taught history* since *1980*.
  Before that, *I taught geography*.

Do you still *live on Main Street*?
  No. I haven't *lived on Main Street for several years*.
Where do you *live* NOW?
  I *live on River Road*.

Are you still *a barber*?
  No. I haven't been *a barber for several years*.
What do you do NOW?
  I'm a *taxi driver*.

So how are you feeling today, *George*?
  Not very well, *Dr. Fernando*.
What seems to be the problem?
  My neck is stiff.

What is your present address?
How long have you lived there?
What was your last address?
How long did you live there?

Tell me, _____.
Tell me, *Tony*, _____.
And how about YOU?

Responding to Information

Really?

Oh, really? That's interesting.

Indicating Understanding

I see.

Greeting People

George!
  Tony!

How have you been?
  Fine. And how about YOU?
Everything's fine with me, too.

Expressing Surprise-Disbelief

I can't believe it's you!

Expressing Agreement

That's right, *George*.

Leave Taking

Well, *George*, I'm afraid I have to go now. We should
  get together soon.
  Good idea, *Tony*.

Present Perfect
Continuous Tense ■

How Long Have You Been Waiting?

(I have)	I've	
(We have)	We've	
(You have)	You've	
(They have)	They've	} been working.
(He has)	He's	
(She has)	She's	
(It has)	It's	

A. How long have you been waiting?

B. I've been waiting for two hours.

A. How long has Henry been working at the post office?

B. He's been working at the post office since 1957.

1. How long have you been feeling bad?

since **yesterday morning**

2. How long has Nancy been playing the piano?

for **several years**

62

3. How long has the phone been ringing? *It's*

for **five minutes**

4. How long have Mr. and Mrs. Brown been living on Appleton Street? *They've*

Since **1948**

5. How long has Maria been studying English? *She's*

for **ten months**

6. How long has Frank been going out with Sally? *he's*

for her **three and a half years**

7. How long have you been having problems with your back? *I've*

Since **high school**

8. How long have we been driving? *we've*

for **seven hours**

9. How long has it been snowing? *it's*

Since **late last night**

10. How long has your baby son been crying? *He's* *He's*

Since **early this morning**

11. How long have they been building the new bridge? *'ve*

for **two years**

12. How long has Arnold been lying in the sun? *He's*

Since **twelve noon**

63

They've Been Arguing All Day

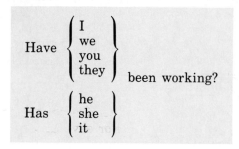

Have { I / we / you / they } been working?

Has { he / she / it }

A. What are your neighbors doing?
B. They're arguing.
A. Have they been arguing for a long time?
B. Yes, they have. They've been arguing all day.*

*Or: They've been arguing all morning/all afternoon/all evening/all night.

1. *you*
   studying

2. *Robert*
   ironing

3. *Laura*
   waiting for the bus

4. *you and your friends*
   standing in line for
   concert tickets

5. *Ricky*
   talking to his girlfriend

6. *Jane*
   looking for her keys

7. *your car*
   making strange noises

8. *Mr. and Mrs. Wilson*
   watching MTV†

9.

†A cable television channel that shows music videos.

APARTMENT PROBLEMS

Mr. and Mrs. Banks have been having a lot of problems in their apartment recently. For several weeks their bedroom ceiling has been leaking, their refrigerator hasn't been working, and the paint in their hallway has been peeling. In addition, they have been taking cold showers since last week because their water heater hasn't been working, and they haven't been sleeping at night because their radiators have been making strange noises.

Mr. and Mrs. Banks are furious. They have been calling their landlord every day and complaining about their problems. He has been promising to help them, but they have been waiting for more than a week, and he still hasn't fixed anything at all.

CHECK-UP

Q & A

Mr. and Mrs. Banks are calling their landlord for the first time about each of the problems in their apartment. Using this model, create dialogs based on the story.

A. Hello.
B. Hello. This is *Mrs.* Banks.
A. Yes, *Mrs.* Banks. What can I do for you?
B. We're having a problem with *our bedroom ceiling.*
A. Oh? What's the problem?
B. *It's leaking.*
A. I see. Tell me, how long *has it been leaking?*
B. *It's been leaking for about an hour.*
A. All right, *Mrs.* Banks. I'll take care of it as soon as I can.
B. Thank you.

How about YOU?

Have you been having problems in your apartment or house recently? Tell about some problems you've been having.

No Wonder They're Tired!

A. You look tired.* What have you been doing?

B. I've been writing letters since ten o'clock this morning.

A. Really? How many letters have you written?

B. Believe it or not, I've already written fifteen letters.

A. Fifteen letters?! NO WONDER you're tired!

A. Mary looks tired.* What has she been doing?

B. She's been baking cakes since nine o'clock this morning.

A. Really? How many cakes has she baked?

B. Believe it or not, she's already baked seven cakes.

A. Seven cakes?! NO WONDER she's tired!

*Or: exhausted

1. *you*
   wash windows
   washed

2. *Dr. Anderson*
   seeing
   see patients for
   Seen

2 **3.** *Miss Shultz* has she
giving
give piano lessons
given

1 **5.** *you*
picking
pick apples
picked

2 **7.** *your grandmother*
修補 mend mending sale
mended *mend socks*

1 **9.** *you and your friends*
ri vju
被動 *review our English lessons*
reviewing
reviewed

2 **11.** *John*
going
go to job interviews

gone

I **4.** *Mr. and Mrs. Johnson* have
been buying ˈkrɪsməs
They've *buy Christmas presents*
bought

2 **6.** *Mr. Williams* He
planting
plant flowers
planted

2 **8.** *Bob*
taking
take photographs
taken

2 **10.** *Jennifer*
writing
write thank-you notes
written

1 **12.** *you*
filling
fill out income tax forms
filled

67

There's Nothing to Be Nervous About!

A. I'm nervous.

B. Why?*

A. I'm going to **fly in an airplane** tomorrow, and I've never **flown in an airplane** before.

B. Don't worry! I've been **flying in airplanes** for years. And believe me, there's nothing to be nervous about!

*Or: How come?

1. *buy a used car* bought
buying

2. *go to a job interview* gone
going to

3. *drive† downtown* driven
driving

4. *give blood* given
giving

5. *take a karate lesson* taken
taking
†drive–drove–driven

6. *speak at a meeting* spoken
speaking

7. do a Chemistry experiment 化學實驗 *kɛmistri is pɛrimənt* done doing

8. sing* in front of an audience 觀眾 *ɔ diəns* sung singing

9. run† in a marathon 長程賽跑 *mæ rə θɑn* run running

10. ask for a raise 加薪 *rez* asked asking

11. go out on a date 幽會 gone going

12.

How about YOU?

Have you ever flown in an airplane?
(Where did you go?)

Have you ever been in the hospital?
(Why were you there?)

Have you ever met a famous person?
(Who did you meet?)

Have you ever spoken at a meeting?
(Where did you speak? What did you say?)

Have you ever been very embarrassed?
(What happened?)

Have you ever been in an accident?
(What happened?)

Now create new questions and ask other students in your class.

*sing–sang–sung
†run–ran–run

ON YOUR OWN: At the Doctor's Office

Complete this conversation and act it out with another student in your class.

A. How are you feeling, (Mr./Mrs./Miss/Ms.) _____?

B. Well, Doctor. I've been having problems with my _____.

A. I'm sorry to hear that. How long have you been having these problems with your _____?

B. (For/Since) _____.

A. Have you ever had problems with your _____ before?

B. No. Never. This is the first time.

A. Tell me, (Mr./Mrs./Miss/Ms.) _____, have you been sleeping okay?

B. No, Doctor. I haven't had a good night's sleep since my _____ began to bother me.

A. And how about your appetite? Have you been eating well lately?

B. ⎰ Yes, I have. ⎱
       ⎱ No, I haven't. ⎰

A. What have you been eating?

B. Well . . . let me see . . . I've been eating _____.

(after the examination)

A. Well, (Mr./Mrs./Miss/Ms.) _____, I think you should _____.*

B. Do you think that will help?

A. Yes, indeed. A lot of people have been coming to me lately with _____ problems, and I've been advising all of them to _____.

B. Thank you, Doctor. You've been a great help.

A. It's been a pleasure, (Mr./Mrs./Miss/Ms.) _____. I'm sure you'll be feeling better soon.

*Some common medical advice: take aspirin three times a day; exercise more; drink a lot of water; rest in bed for a few days; see a specialist.

IT'S BEEN A LONG DAY

Mario has been assembling cameras since 7 A.M., and he's very tired. He has assembled 19 cameras today, and he has NEVER assembled that many cameras in one day before! He has to assemble only one more camera, and then he can go home. He's really glad. It's been a long day.

Judy has been typing letters since 9 A.M., and she's very tired. She has typed 25 letters today, and she has NEVER typed that many letters in one day before! She has to type only one more letter, and then she can go home. She's really glad. It's been a very long day.

Officers Jackson and Parker have been writing parking tickets since 8 A.M., and they're exhausted! They have written 211 parking tickets today, and they have NEVER written that many parking tickets in one day before! They have to write only one more parking ticket, and then they can go home. They're really glad. It's been an extremely long day.

CHECK-UP

IN YOUR OWN WORDS

Listening

I. Listen and decide who is speaking.

1. a. a landlord   b. a boss
2. a. a teacher   b. a student
3. a. a policeman   b. a movie theater cashier
4. a. a window washer   b. a baby-sitter
5. a. a singer   b. a teacher
6. a. a doctor   b. a bookkeeper

II. Listen and choose the word you hear.

1. a. gone   b. going
2. a. written   b. writing
3. a. seen   b. seeing
4. a. taken   b. taking
5. a. given   b. giving
6. a. driven   b. driving

Tell about yourself.

Where do you live?
How long have you been living there?
Have you lived anywhere else?
Where? How long?

Where do you work or go to school?
How long have you been working or going to school there?

Have you worked or gone to school anywhere else? Where? How long?
What did you do there?
What did you study?

Now interview a friend, a neighbor, or someone in your family and tell the class about this person.

Grammar

Present Perfect Continuous Tense

(I have)	I've	
(We have)	We've	
(You have)	You've	
(They have)	They've	been working.
(He has)	He's	
(She has)	She's	
(It has)	It's	

Have	I we you they	been working?
Has	he she it	

Yes,	I we you they	have.
	he she it	has.

Irregular Verbs

fly– flew –flown
drive–drove–driven
run– ran –run
sing– sang –sung

FUNCTIONS

Asking for and Reporting Information

What have you been doing?
  I've been *writing letters.*
How many *letters* have you *written*?
  I've already *written fifteen letters.*

How long have you been *waiting*?
  I've been *waiting* for *two hours.*
  I've been *waiting* since *twelve noon.*

What *are your neighbors* doing?
  They're arguing.
Have *they* been *arguing* for a long time?
  Yes, *they* have. *They've* been *arguing all day.*

Have you been *sleeping okay*?
Have you been *eating well* lately?

Where do you *live*?
How long have you been *living* there?
Have you *lived* anywhere else?
Where?
How long?

Have you ever *flown in an airplane*?

I'm going to *fly in an airplane tomorrow*, and I've never *flown in an airplane* before.

I've been *flying in airplanes for years.*

How are you feeling?
  I've been having problems with my _____.

We're having a problem with *our bedroom ceiling.*
  Oh? What's the problem?
It's leaking.

Tell me, _____.

Why?
How come?

Responding to Information

Really?

Indicating Understanding

I see.

Expressing Surprise-Disbelief

Fifteen letters?!

Sympathizing

I'm sorry to hear that.

Asking for Advice

Do you think that will help?

Offering Advice

I think you should _____.
I've been advising *all of them* to _____.

Describing Feelings-Emotions

I'm nervous.

Reassuring

Don't worry!

Believe me, there's nothing to be nervous about!

I'm sure you'll be feeling better soon.

Persuading

Believe me, . . .

Expressing Intention

I'll *take care of it* as soon as I can.

Greeting People

Hello.
  Hello. This is *Mrs. Banks.*
Yes, *Mrs. Banks.* What can I do for you?

Initiating a Topic

You look tired.
You look exhausted.

Expressing Gratitude

Thank you.
Thank you, *Doctor.*

You've been a great help.

Responding to Gratitude

It's been a pleasure.

Gerunds ■
Infinitives ■
Review: Present Perfect and
   Present Perfect Continuous
   Tenses ■

My Favorite Way to Relax

to read	reading
to dance	dancing
to swim	swimming

A. Do you **like to watch** TV?

B. Yes. I **enjoy watching** TV very much. **Watching** TV is my favorite way to relax.

1. *you*
listen to music

2. *Tom*
swim

3. *Lucy*
read

4. *you and your friends*
dance

5. *Mr. and Mrs. Green*
play tennis

6. *you*
ice skate

7. *Shirley*
sew

8. *Alan*
play chess

9. *your parents*
go to the movies

READING

ENJOYING LIFE

Howard enjoys reading. He likes to read in the park. He likes to read in the library. He even likes to read in the bathtub! As you can see, reading is a very important part of Howard's life.

Patty enjoys singing. She likes to sing in school. She likes to sing in church. She even likes to sing in the shower! As you can see, singing is a very important part of Patty's life.

Brenda enjoys watching TV. She likes to watch TV in the living room. She likes to watch TV in bed. She even likes to watch TV in department stores! As you can see, watching TV is a very important part of Brenda's life.

Tom enjoys talking about politics. He likes to talk about politics with his friends. He likes to talk about politics with his parents. He even likes to talk about politics with his barber! As you can see, talking about politics is a very important part of Tom's life.

CHECK-UP

Q & A

The people in the story are introducing themselves to you at a party. Using this model, create dialogs based on the story.

A. Hello. My name is *Howard*.
B. Nice to meet you, *Howard*. I'm _____.
A. Are you enjoying the party?
B. Yes. How about you?
A. Well, not really. To tell you the truth, I'd rather be *reading*.
B. Oh? Do you like to *read*?
A. Oh, yes. I enjoy *reading* very much. How about you?
B. I like to *read*, too. In fact, *reading* is my favorite way to relax.
A. Mine, too. Tell me, what do you like to *read*?
B. I like to *read books about famous people*. How about you?
A. I enjoy *reading short stories*.
B. Well, please excuse me. I have to go now. It was nice meeting you, *Howard*.
A. Nice meeting you, too, _____.

He Can't Stand to Travel by Plane

| like to work
like working | can't stand to work
can't stand working | —
avoid working |

A. Does Ronald **like** { to travel / traveling } by plane?

B. No. He **can't stand** { to travel / traveling }* by plane.

He **avoids traveling** by plane whenever he can.

*Or: hates { to travel / traveling }

1. *Sally*
   do her homework

2. *Mr. and Mrs. Simon*
   drive downtown

3. *you*
   talk on the telephone

4. *Jim*
   work late at the office

5. *you and your friends*
   talk about politics

6. *Julie*
   eat spinach

7. *you*
   sit in the sun

8. *Michael*
   visit his mother-in-law

9. *Mr. and Mrs. Kendall*
   play cards with their neighbors

How about YOU?

What do you enjoy doing?
What do you avoid doing whenever you can?

BAD HABITS

Harriet's friends always tell her to stop smoking. They think that smoking is unhealthy. Harriet knows that, but she still keeps on smoking. She wants to stop, but she can't. Smoking is a habit she just can't break.

Vincent's friends always tell him to stop gossiping. They think that gossiping isn't nice. Vincent knows that, but he still keeps on gossiping. He wants to stop, but he can't. Gossiping is a habit he just can't break.

Jennifer's mother always tells her to stop interrupting people while they're talking. She thinks that interrupting people is very rude. Jennifer knows that, but she still keeps on interrupting people. She wants to stop, but she can't. Interrupting people is a habit she just can't break.

Walter's wife always tells him to stop talking about business all the time. She thinks that talking about business all the time is boring. Walter knows that, but he still keeps on talking about business. He wants to stop, but he can't. Talking about business is a habit he just can't break.

CHECK-UP

Q & A

You're talking with the people in this story about their bad habits. Using this model, create dialogs based on the story.

A. *Harriet?*
B. Yes?
A. You know . . . I don't mean to be critical, but I really think you should stop *smoking*.
B. Oh?
A. Yes. *Smoking is unhealthy.* Don't you think so?
B. You're right. The truth is . . . I want to stop, but I can't. *Smoking* is a habit I just can't break.

How about YOU?

Do you have any habits you "just can't break"?
Tell about them.

How Did You Learn to Swim So Well?

$\begin{Bmatrix} \textbf{start to } \text{swim} \\ \textbf{start } \text{swim}\textbf{ing} \end{Bmatrix}$ $\begin{Bmatrix} \textbf{learn to } \text{swim} \\ — \end{Bmatrix}$ $\begin{Bmatrix} — \\ \textbf{practice } \text{swimming} \end{Bmatrix}$

A. How did you **learn to swim** so well?

B. Well, I **started** $\begin{Bmatrix} \textbf{to swim} \\ \textbf{swimming} \end{Bmatrix}$ when I was young,

and I've been **swimming** ever since.

A. I envy you. I've never **swum** before.

B. I'll be glad to teach you how.

A. Thank you.* But isn't **swimming** very difficult?

B. Not at all. After you **practice swimming** a few times, you'll probably **swim** as well as I do.

*Or: I appreciate that. That's very kind of you. That's very nice of you.

A. How did you learn to _____ so well?

B. Well, I started { to _____ / _____ing } when I was young, and I've been _____ing ever since.

A. I envy you. I've never _____ before.

B. I'll be glad to teach you how.

A. Thank you.* But isn't _____ing very difficult?

B. Not at all. After you practice _____ing a few times, you'll probably _____ as well as I do.

*Or: I appreciate that. That's very kind of you. That's very nice of you.

1. *draw†*

2. *ski*

3. *figure skate*

4. *surf*

5. *dance*

6. *use a computer*

7. *box*

8.

†**draw–drew–drawn**

Guess What I've Decided to Do!

$$\left\{\begin{array}{l}\textbf{decide to } \text{buy}\\ -\end{array}\right\} \quad \left\{\begin{array}{l}-\\ \textbf{consider } \text{buying}\end{array}\right\} \quad \left\{\begin{array}{l}-\\ \textbf{think about } \text{buying}\end{array}\right\}$$

A. Guess what I've decided to do!

B. What?

A. I've **decided to get married**.

B. You HAVE? That's GREAT! Tell me, how long have you been **thinking about getting married**?

A. For a long time, actually. I **considered getting married** YEARS ago, but never did. Do you think I'm making the right decision?

B. Absolutely! I think **getting married** is a WONDERFUL idea!

A. I'm glad you think so.

A. Guess what I've decided to do!

B. What?

A. I've decided to _____.

B. You HAVE? That's GREAT! Tell me, how long have you been thinking about _____ing?

A. For a long time, actually. I considered _____ing YEARS ago, but never did. Do you think I'm making the right decision?

B. Absolutely! I think _____ing is a WONDERFUL idea!

A. I'm glad you think so.

1. *move to Chicago*

2. *buy a new car*

3. *get a dog*

4. *go on a diet*

5. *grow* a beard*

6. *go back to college*

7. *start my own business*

8. *become a vegetarian*

9.

*grow–grew–grown

ON YOUR OWN: I Have Some Good News!

{ start **to** eat / start eating }	{ continue **to** eat / continue eating }	{ — / stop eating }
{ begin **to** eat / begin eating }	{ — / keep on eating }	{ — / quit eating }

Complete this conversation and practice with another student.

A. I have some good news!

B. What?

A. I've decided to stop* _____ing.

B. That's GREAT! Do you really think you'll be able to do it?

A. I think so. But it won't be easy. I've been _____ing for a long time.

B. Have you ever tried to stop _____ing before?

A. Yes. Many times. But every time I've stopped _____ing,

I've started† { to _____ / _____ing } again after a few days.

B. I hope you're successful this time.

A. I hope so, too. After all, I can't keep on** _____ing for the rest of my life!

*Or: quit
†Or: begun (**begin–began–begun**)
**Or: continue

1. *eat junk food*

2. *tease my brother*

3. *worry about my health*

4.

IMPORTANT DECISIONS

Jim had to make an important decision recently. He made an appointment for an interview at the Acme Insurance Company, and he had to decide what to wear. First, he considered wearing a sweater to the interview. Then, he thought about wearing a sports jacket. Finally, he decided to wear a suit and tie. Jim thinks he made the right decision. He's glad he didn't wear a sweater or sports jacket. He feels that wearing a suit and tie was the best thing for him to do.

Lana had to make an important decision recently. Her landlord sold her apartment building, and she had to decide where to move. First, she considered moving to another apartment. Then, she thought about buying a small house. Finally, she decided to move home with her parents for a while. Lana thinks she made the right decision. She's glad she didn't move to another apartment or buy a small house. She feels that moving home with her parents for a while was the right thing for her to do.

Nick had to make an important decision recently. He got out of the army, and he had to decide what to do next with his life. First, he considered working in his family's grocery store. Then, he thought about taking a job in a restaurant. Finally, he decided to enroll in college and study engineering. Nick thinks he made the right decision. He's glad he didn't work in his family's grocery store or take a job in a restaurant. He feels that enrolling in college and studying engineering was the smartest thing for him to do.

Maria had to make an important decision recently. She lost her job as a bookkeeper because her company went out of business, and she had to decide what to do. First, she considered looking for another job as a bookkeeper. Then, she thought about working as a secretary for a while. Finally, she decided to enroll in technical school and study computer programming. Maria thinks she made the right decision. She's glad she didn't look for another job as a bookkeeper or work as a secretary for a while. She feels that enrolling in technical school and studying computer programming was the best thing for her to do.

 CHECK-UP

True, False, or Maybe?

Answer True, False, or Maybe (if the answer isn't in the story).

1. Jim considered wearing a sweater to the interview.
2. He got the job at the Acme Insurance Company.
3. Lana decided not to move to another apartment.
4. Lana never considered buying a small house.
5. Lana's parents think that moving home was the right thing for Lana to do.
6. Nick's family is in the restaurant business.
7. Nick first became interested in engineering while he was in the army.
8. Maria wasn't a very good bookkeeper.
9. After Maria lost her job, she worked as a secretary for a while.
10. Maria feels she made the right decision.

Q & A

The people in the story are asking you for advice about the decisions they have to make. Using this model, create dialogs based on the story.

A. Can I ask you a question?
B. Sure.
A. I need some advice. *I've* just *made an appointment for a job interview at the Acme Insurance Company*, and now I have to decide *what to wear*.
B. Hmm. That's an important decision.
A. It is. I've considered *wearing a sweater*. I've also been thinking about *wearing a sports jacket*. But I'm not really sure. What do you think?
B. Well . . . Have you considered *wearing a suit and tie*?
A. No. That's a good idea. I'll think about it. Thanks.

Choose

I.

1. Can you ____ me how?
   a. practice
   b. teach

2. Playing chess is my ____ way to relax.
   a. enjoy
   b. favorite

3. Gossiping is a bad ____.
   a. habit
   b. rude

4. I'm not sure what to do. Do you have any good ____?
   a. decisions
   b. suggestions

5. I ____ you.
   a. enroll
   b. envy

6. Please don't ____ our conversation.
   a. interrupt
   b. break

II.

1. My sister ____ traveling by train.
   a. likes to
   b. enjoys

2. Jimmy ____ to do his homework.
   a. avoids
   b. can't stand

3. I've ____ to go on a diet.
   a. decided
   b. considered

4. I ____ swim when I was three years old.
   a. began
   b. started to

5. ____ is an important decision.
   a. Buying a house
   b. Buy a house

6. I know I shouldn't ____ eat junk food.
   a. continue to
   b. keep on

Listening

Listen and choose the best answer.

1. a. He enjoys driving downtown.
   b. He hates driving downtown.

2. a. She sold her car.
   b. She's going to sell her car.

3. a. He bites his nails.
   b. He stopped biting his nails.

4. a. They're going to move to California.
   b. They might move to California.

5. a. He's married.
   b. He isn't married.

6. a. She's going to keep on practicing.
   b. She isn't going to continue practicing.

IN YOUR OWN WORDS

For Writing and Discussion

AN IMPORTANT DECISION

Tell a story about an important decision you had to make.

I had to make an important decision recently. _____, and I had to decide what to do. First, I considered _____. Then, I thought about _____. Finally, I decided to _____. I'm glad I didn't _____ or _____. I feel that _____ was the best thing for me to do.

GRAMMAR

Infinitives
Gerunds

I	like can't stand started began continue	to work. working.

I	enjoy avoid considered keep on practice stopped quit	-------------
	I'm thinking about	swimming.

I learned I decided	to swim. ------------

------------------	is my favorite way
Watching TV	to relax.

FUNCTIONS

Inquiring about Likes/Dislikes

Do you like to *watch* TV?

What do you like to *read?*

Expressing Likes

I enjoy *reading short stories.*
I enjoy *watching* TV very much.
I like to *read books about famous people.*

Watching TV is my favorite way to *relax.*

Expressing Dislikes

I can't stand *to talk on the telephone.*
I can't stand *talking on the telephone.*

I avoid *sitting in the sun* whenever I can.

Inquiring about Satisfaction

Are you enjoying the *party?*

Expressing Preference

I'd rather *be reading.*

Asking for Advice

I need some advice.

What do you think?

Do you think I'm making the right decision?

I have to decide *what to wear.*

Offering Advice

I don't mean to be critical, but I really think you should stop *smoking.*

I think *getting married* is a WONDERFUL idea!

Have you considered *wearing a suit and tie?*

Responding to Advice

That's a good idea.

I'll think about it.

Initiating a Topic

Guess what I've decided to do!

I have some good news!

Asking for and Reporting Information

Tell me, _____.

Can I ask you a question?

How about you?

I've never *swum* before.

I've decided to *get married.*

I considered *getting married* YEARS *ago,* but never did.

I've considered *wearing a sweater.*
I've been thinking about *wearing a sports jacket.*

I've been *eating junk food* for a long time.

How long have you been thinking about *getting married?*

How did you learn to *swim* so well? I started to *swim* when I was *young,* and I've been *swimming* ever since.

Have you ever tried to *stop eating junk food* before?

Responding to Information

I'm glad you think so.

Focusing Attention

In fact, . . .

After all, . . .

Admitting

To tell you the truth, . . .

The truth is, . . .

Congratulating

That's GREAT!

Inquiring about Agreement

Don't you think so?

Expressing Agreement

You're right.

Absolutely!

Expressing Gratitude

Thank you.
Thanks.

I appreciate that.
That's very kind of you.
That's very nice of you.

Describing Feelings-Emotions

I envy you.

Hesitating

You know . . .

Attracting Attention

Harriet?

Past Perfect Tense ▪
Past Perfect Continuous Tense ▪

They Didn't Want To

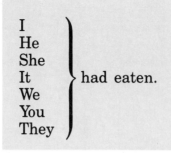

I
He
She
It
We
You
They
} had eaten.

the weekend before

A. Did Mr. and Mrs. Jones **drive** to the beach last weekend?

B. No. They didn't want to. They **had** just **driven** to the beach the weekend before.

the night before

1. Did Mr. and Mrs. Henderson see a movie last Saturday night?

the evening before

2. Did George eat out yesterday evening?

the day before

3. Did Billy fly* his kite yesterday?

the weekend before

4. Did you go canoeing last weekend?

*fly–flew–flown

the Sunday before

5. Did you and your friends have a picnic last Sunday?

the night before

6. Did Shirley have pizza for dinner last night?

the year before

7. Did Gregory take a geography course last year?

the weekend before

8. Did Helen give a party last weekend?

the evening before

9. Did Mr. and Mrs. Stevens discuss politics at the dinner table yesterday evening?

the day before

10. Did you go window-shopping last Saturday?

the week before

11. Did Mabel bake one of her delicious apple pies last week?

the day before

12. Did Philip wear his polka dot shirt to work last Tuesday?

the weekend before

13. Did Barry do magic tricks for his friends last weekend?

14.

THE MOST IMPORTANT THING

Roger thought he was all prepared for his dinner party last night. He had sent invitations to his boss and all the people at the office. He had looked through several cookbooks and had found some very interesting recipes. He had even gone all the way downtown to buy imported fruit, vegetables, and cheese, which he needed for his dinner. However, as soon as Roger's doorbell rang and his guests arrived, he realized that he had forgotten to turn on the oven. Roger felt very foolish. He couldn't believe what he had done. He thought he was all prepared for his dinner party, but he had forgotten to do the most important thing.

Mr. and Mrs. Jenkins thought they were all prepared for their vacation. They had packed their suitcases several days ahead of time. They had gone to the bank and purchased travelers checks. They had even asked their next-door neighbor to water their plants, feed their dog, and shovel their driveway in case it snowed. However, as soon as Mr. and Mrs. Jenkins arrived at the airport, they realized that they had forgotten to bring their plane tickets with them, and there wasn't enough time to go back home and get them. Mr. and Mrs. Jenkins were heartbroken. They couldn't believe what they had done. They thought they were all prepared for their vacation, but they had forgotten to do the most important thing.

Harold thought he was all prepared for his job interview yesterday. He had gone to his barber and gotten a very short haircut. He had bought a new shirt, put on his best tie, and shined his shoes. He had even borrowed his brother's new suit. However, as soon as Harold began the job interview, he realized that he had forgotten to bring along his resume. Harold was furious with himself. He thought he was all prepared for his job interview, but he had forgotten to do the most important thing.

Janet thought she was all prepared for the school play. She had memorized the script several weeks in advance. She had practiced her songs and dances until she knew them perfectly. She had even stayed up all night the night before and rehearsed the play by herself from beginning to end. However, as soon as the curtain went up and the play began last night, Janet realized that she had forgotten to put on her costume. Janet was really embarrassed. She couldn't believe what she had done. She thought she was all prepared for the play, but she had forgotten to do the most important thing.

CHECK-UP

True, False, or Maybe?

Answer True, False, or Maybe (if the answer isn't in the story).

1. Roger hadn't remembered to cook the food.
2. Roger's guests couldn't believe what he had done.
3. Mr. and Mrs. Jenkins had forgotten to buy their plane tickets.
4. When Mr. and Mrs. Jenkins realized what had happened, they felt very sad and upset.
5. Harold thinks it's important to bring a resume to a job interview.
6. Harold doesn't have a suit.
7. Janet hadn't seen the script until the night before the play.
8. Before the play began, Janet hadn't realized that she had forgotten to put on her costume.

Choose

1. Before Barbara went on her vacation, she went to the bank and bought
   | tickets |
   | travelers checks |
   .

2. Peter wanted his boss to come over for dinner, but he forgot to send
   him | a resume |
   | an invitation |
   .

3. Sheila | borrowed |
   | bought |
   her roommate's

   typewriter for a few days.

4. Our grandchildren were | heartbroken |
   | foolish |

   when our dog ran away.

5. At the supermarket next to the United

   Nations, | imported |
   | important |
   people buy

   | imported |
   | important |
   food.

How about YOU?

Have you ever thought you were all prepared for something, but then you realized you had forgotten to do something important?
    What were you preparing for?
    What had you done?
    What had you forgotten to do?

They Didn't Get There on Time

A. Did you get to the **plane** on time?

B. No, I didn't. By the time I got to the **plane,** it had already **taken off.**

1. concert
   begin

2. post office
   close

3. train
   leave

4. lecture
   end

5. movie
   start

6. meeting
   finish

7. bank
   close

8. boat
   sail away

9. parade
   go by

He Hadn't Seen His Old Friends in a Long Time

I
He
She
It
We
You
They
} hadn't eaten.
(had not)

A. Did George enjoy **seeing his old friends** last night?

B. Yes, he did. He hadn't **seen his old friends** in a long time.

1. Did you enjoy swimming in the ocean last weekend?

2. Did Janice enjoy singing with the choir last Sunday?

3. Did Mr. and Mrs. Gleason enjoy taking a walk along the beach yesterday?

4. Did you and your friends enjoy going out for dinner last night?

5. Did Susan enjoy visiting her grandparents last Sunday afternoon?

6. Did Andrew and Eric enjoy having chocolate cake for dessert last night?

7. Did Professor Nelson enjoy seeing his former students last week?

8. Did Walter enjoy playing "hide and seek" with his children last night?

9. Did Mrs. Thompson enjoy reading her old love letters last weekend?

DAYS GONE BY

Michael took a very special trip last month. He went back to Fullerton, his home town. Michael's visit to Fullerton was very special to him. He was born there, he grew up there, but he hadn't been back there since he finished high school.

He went to places he hadn't gone to in years. He walked through the park in the center of town and remembered the days he had walked through that same park with his first girlfriend. He passed by the empty field where he and his friends had played baseball every day after school. And he stood for a while in front of the movie theater and thought about all the Saturday afternoons he had spent there sitting in the balcony, watching his favorite movie heroes and eating popcorn.

He did things he hadn't done in a long time. He had some homemade ice cream at the ice cream shop, he rode on the merry-go-round in the park, and he went fishing at the lake on the outskirts of town. For a little while, he felt like a kid again. He hadn't had homemade ice cream, ridden on a merry-go-round, or gone fishing since he was a young boy.

He also saw people he hadn't seen in years. He visited several of his old neighbors who had never moved out of the neighborhood. He said hello to the owners of the candy store near his house. And he even bumped into Mrs. Riley, his tenth-grade science teacher!

During his visit to his home town, Michael remembered places he hadn't gone to, things he hadn't done, and people he hadn't seen since his childhood. Michael's trip back to Fullerton was a very nostalgic experience for him. Going back to Fullerton brought back many memories of days gone by.

True, False, or Maybe?

Answer True, False, or Maybe (if the answer isn't in the story).

1. Michael moved back to Fullerton last month.
2. He hadn't seen Fullerton in years.
3. When Michael passed by the field last month, children were playing baseball.
4. Michael enjoyed going to the movies when he was young.
5. The ice cream shop was near Michael's home in Fullerton.
6. Michael rode on the merry-go-round when he was a young boy.
7. Some of Michael's old neighbors still live in the same neighborhood.
8. Mrs. Riley still teaches science.

Choose

What word doesn't belong?

1. a. river	b. ocean	c. park	d. lake
2. a. evening	b. before	c. weekend	d. week
3. a. movies	b. candy	c. ice cream	d. popcorn
4. a. end	b. finish	c. close	d. start
5. a. resume	b. invitation	c. interview	d. script
6. a. prepare	b. rehearse	c. realize	d. memorize

Listening

Listen and choose the best answer.

1. a. Did you like it?
   b. When are you going to see it?

2. a. Did you enjoy it?
   b. Why not?

3. a. It had already started.
   b. It has already begun.

4. a. But I had already done it.
   b. But I've already done it.

5. a. She had memorized all the important names and dates.
   b. She's going to study very hard.

6. a. Had you ever eaten there before?
   b. Have you ever eaten there?

How about YOU?

Tell about feelings you have had.

I feel nostalgic when . . . .
I felt foolish when . . . .
I was furious when . . . .
I was heartbroken when . . . .

Have You Heard About Harry?

A. Have you heard about Harry?

B. No, I haven't. What happened?

A. He broke his leg last week.

B. That's terrible! How did he do THAT?

A. He was playing soccer . . . and he had never played soccer before.

B. Poor Harry! I hope he feels better soon.

A. Have you heard about _____?

B. No, I haven't. What happened?

A. (He/She) _____ last week.

B. That's terrible! How did (he/she) do THAT?

A. (He/She) was _____ing . . . and (he/she) had never _____ before.

B. Poor _____! I hope (he/she) feels better soon.

1. *twist his ankle*
   fly a kite

2. *sprain her wrist*
   play tennis

3. *burn himself*
   bake chocolate chip cookies

4. *get hurt in an accident*
   ride on a motorcycle

5. *get a black eye*
   box

6. *injure her knee*
   wrestle

7. *break his front teeth*
   chew on a steak bone

8. *lose her voice*
   sing opera

9. *sprain his back*
   do the tango

10.

It's Really a Shame

I He She It We You They	had been eating.

A. I heard that Arnold failed his driver's test last week. Is it true?

B. Yes, it is . . . and it's really a shame. He had been practicing for a long time.

A. I heard that _____ last week.
Is it true?

B. Yes, it is . . . and it's really a shame.
(He/She/They) had been _____ing for a long time.

I heard that . . .

1. Lucy lost her job at the bank
   work there

2. Boris lost the chess match
   practice

98

3. Ted and Carol broke up
   go together

4. Robert did poorly on his English examination
   study for it

5. Sally had to cancel her trip to Canada
   plan it

6. Dick and Janet canceled their wedding
   plan to get married

7. Mrs. Gold had another heart attack
   feel better

8. Mr. and Mrs. Hardy moved
   live in this neighborhood

9. Lisa got sick and couldn't see the parade
   hope to see it

10. Roger caught a cold and couldn't go camping
    look forward to it

NOBODY WAS SURPRISED

When Stella Karp won the marathon last week, nobody was surprised. She had been getting up early and jogging every morning. She had been eating health foods and taking vitamins for several months. And she had been swimming fifty laps every day after work. Stella Karp really deserved to win the marathon. After all, she had been preparing for it for a long time.

When my friend Stuart finally passed his driver's test the other day, nobody was surprised. He had been taking lessons at the driving school for several months. He had been practicing driving with his father for the past several weeks. And he had been studying the "rules of the road" in the driver's manual since he was a little boy. My friend Stuart really deserved to pass his driver's test. After all, he had been preparing for it for a long time.

When Sally Compton got a promotion last week, nobody was surprised. She had been working overtime every day for several months. She had been studying computer programming in the evening. And she had even been taking extra work home on the weekends. Sally Compton really deserved to get a promotion. After all, she had been working hard to earn it for a long time.

IN YOUR OWN WORDS

For Writing and Discussion

We shouldn't be surprised when we accomplish something that we have worked for. Tell a story about something you accomplished.

What did you accomplish?
How long had you been preparing for that?
How had you been preparing?

1. Patty had planned to have a party last weekend. She had been getting ready for the party for a long time. She had invited all of her friends, she had cooked lots of food, and she had cleaned her apartment from top to bottom. But at the last minute, she got sick and had to cancel her party. Poor Patty! She was really disappointed.

2. Michael had planned to ask his boss for a raise last week. He had been preparing to ask his boss for a raise for a long time. He had come to work early for several weeks, he had worked late at the office every night, and he had even bought a new suit to wear to the appointment with his boss. Unfortunately, before Michael could even ask for a raise, his boss fired him.

3. John and Julia had planned to get married last month. They had been planning their wedding for several months, and all of their friends and relatives had been looking forward to the ceremony. Julia had bought a beautiful wedding gown, John had rented a fancy tuxedo, and they had sent invitations to 150 people. But at the last minute, John "got cold feet"* and they had to cancel the wedding.

Talk with other students about plans YOU had that "fell through."

What had you planned to do?
How long had you been planning to do it?
What had you done beforehand?
What went wrong? (What happened?)
Were you upset? disappointed?

*Or: got scared

CHAPTER 8 *SUMMARY*

GRAMMAR

Past Perfect Tense

I He She It We You They	had eaten.

I He She It We You They	hadn't eaten.

Past Perfect Continuous Tense

I He She It We You They	had been eating.

FUNCTIONS

Asking for and Reporting Information

I heard that *Arnold failed his driver's test.*

Have you heard about *Harry?*

What happened?
What went wrong?

He *broke* his *leg.*
She *sprained* her *wrist.*

How did *he* do that?

He was *playing soccer*. . . and he had never *played soccer* before.

I hadn't *swum in the ocean* in a long time.

Did *Mr. and Mrs. Jones drive to the beach last weekend?*
No.   *They* had just *driven to the beach the weekend before.*

Did you *get to the plane* on time?
No, I didn't.   By the time *I got to the plane, it* had already *taken off.*

What were you preparing for?
What had you done?
What had you forgotten to do?
What had you planned to do?
What had you done beforehand?
How long had you been planning to do it?
How long had you been preparing for that?
What did you accomplish?

Is it true?
Yes, it is.

Responding to Information

That's terrible!

Sympathizing

Poor *Harry!*

Expressing Regret

It's really a shame.

Expressing Hope

I hope *he feels better soon.*

Inquiring about Feelings-Emotions

Were you upset?
Were you disappointed?

Describing Feelings-Emotions

I feel nostalgic when _____.
I felt foolish when _____.
I was furious when _____.
I was heartbroken when _____.

Inquiring about Satisfaction

Did you enjoy *swimming last weekend?*

Expressing Want-Desire

They didn't want to.

Two-Word Verbs:
Separable ■
Inseparable ■

Sometime Next Week

> bring **back** the TV   **bring** it **back**
> **call up** Sally   **call** her **up**
> **put away** the clothes   **put** them **away**

A. When is the repairman going to **bring back** your TV?

B. He's going to **bring** it **back** sometime next week.

1. When are you going to **call up** your cousin in Chicago?

2. When is Peter going to **fill out** his college application forms?

3. When is Greta going to **pick up** her clothes at the cleaner's?

4. When is Maria going to **pick out** her wedding gown?

5. When are you going to **put away** your winter clothes?

6. When is Brian going to **take back** his library books?

7. When is your landlord going to **turn on** the heat?

8. When is Margaret going to **throw out** her old magazines?

9. When are you going to **hang up** your new portrait?

I Completely Forgot!

$$\begin{Bmatrix} \textbf{put on} \text{ your boots} \\ \textbf{put} \text{ your boots } \textbf{on} \end{Bmatrix} \quad \textbf{put} \text{ them } \textbf{on}$$

A. Did you remember to $\begin{Bmatrix} \textbf{turn off} \text{ the oven} \\ \textbf{turn} \text{ the oven } \textbf{off} \end{Bmatrix}$?

B. Oh, no! I completely forgot! I'll **turn** it **off** right away.

1. *take back*
   your library books

2. *put away*
   your toys

3. *call up*
   your Aunt Gertrude

4. *fill out*
   the accident report

5. *hand in*
   your English homework

6. *take out*
   the garbage

7. *take off*
   your boots

8. *put on*
   your raincoat

9. *turn on*
   the "No Smoking"
   sign

A BUSY SATURDAY

Everybody in the Martini family is very busy today. It's Saturday, and they all have to do the things they didn't do during the week.

Mr. Martini has to fill out his income tax form. He didn't have time to fill it out during the week.

Mrs. Martini has to pick up her clothes at the cleaner's. She was too busy to pick them up during the week.

Their son Frank has to throw out all the old magazines and newspapers in the garage. He didn't have time to throw them out during the week.

Their other son, Bob, has to take his library books back. He forgot to take them back during the week.

And their daughter, Julie, has to put her toys away. She didn't feel like putting them away during the week.

As you can see, everybody in the Martini family is going to be very busy today.

✓CHECK-UP

Q & A

You're inviting somebody in the Martini family to do something with you. Using this model, create dialogs based on the story.

A. Would you like to *go fishing* this morning?
B. I'd like to, but I can't. I have to *fill out my income tax form.*
A. That's too bad.
B. I know, but I've really got to do it. I *didn't have time to fill it out* during the week.
A. Well, maybe some other time.
B. Okay.

How about YOU?

What do you have to do on your next day off from work or school?

I Don't Think So

A. Do you think I should keep these old love letters?

B. No. I don't think so. I think you should **throw** them **away.**

1. *keep my ex-boyfriend's ring*
   give back

2. *leave the air conditioner on*
   turn off

3. *hand my homework in*
   do over

4. *erase all my mistakes*
   cross out

5. *use up this old milk*
   throw out

6. *try to remember Sally's telephone number*
   write down

7. *make my decision right away*
   think over

8. *accept my new job offer*
   turn down

9. *ask the teacher the definition of this new word*
   look up

LUCY'S ENGLISH COMPOSITION

Lucy is very discouraged. She handed in her English composition this morning, but her English teacher gave it right back to her and told her to do it over. Apparently, her English teacher didn't like the way she had done it. She hadn't erased her mistakes. She had simply crossed them out. Also, she had used several words incorrectly, since she hadn't looked them up in the dictionary. And finally, she hadn't written her homework on the correct paper because she had accidentally thrown her notebook away. Poor Lucy! She didn't feel like writing her English composition in the first place, and now she has to do it over!

✔ CHECK-UP

What's the Word?

Choose the correct words to complete the sentences.

do over	give back	hand in	look up	throw away

1. I need the dictionary you borrowed from me. Please _____ _____ _____.
2. I want to check your homework. Please _____ _____ _____.
3. Ms. Smith, there are too many mistakes in this letter. Please _____ _____ _____.
4. I haven't read today's newspaper yet. Please don't _____ _____ _____.
5. I don't remember his phone number. Please _____ _____ _____.

Listening: *DEAR ALICE*

Listen and write the missing words.

Dear Alice,

I'm very discouraged. I'm having a lot of trouble with my girlfriend, and I don't know what to do. The problem is very simple. I'm in love with her, but she isn't in love with me! A few weeks ago I gave her a ring, but she _____. During the past few months I have written several love letters to her, but she has _____. Recently I asked her to marry me. She _____ for a while, and then she _____. Now when I try to _____ she doesn't even want to talk to me. Please try to help me. I don't know what to do.

"Discouraged Donald"
Denver, Colorado

What should "Discouraged Donald" do? **Write an answer to his letter.**

Would You Like to Get Together Today?

Hi, Paul. This is Tom. Would you like to get together today?

I'm afraid I can't. I have to **take back** my library books.

Are you free after you **take** them **back**?

I'm afraid not. I also have to **pick** my car **up** at the repair shop.

Would you like to get together after you **pick** it **up**?

I'd really like to, but I can't. I ALSO have to **drop** my sister **off** at the airport.

You're really busy today! What do you have to do after you **drop** her **off**?

Nothing. But by then I'll probably be EXHAUSTED! Let's get together tomorrow instead.

Fine. I'll call you in the morning.

That'll be great. Speak to you then.

A. Hi, _____. This is _____. Would you like to get together today?

B. I'm afraid I can't. I have to _____.

A. Are you free after you _____?

B. I'm afraid not. I also have to _____.

A. Would you like to get together after you _____?

B. I'd really like to, but I can't. I ALSO have to _____.

A. You're really busy today! What do you have to do after you _____?

B. Nothing. But by then I'll probably be EXHAUSTED! Let's get together tomorrow instead.

A. Fine. I'll call you in the morning.

B. That'll be great. Speak to you then.

1.

2.

3.

☑ **take down** my Christmas decorations *take them down.*
☑ **hang up** my New Year's party decorations *hang them up.*
☑ **drop off** my suit at the cleaner's *drop them off.*

4.

I'll get
☑ **figure out** my hospital bill *it*
☑ **fill out** my insurance form *it*
☑ **call up** the doctor *it*

5.

☑ **pick out** my wedding dress *pick it out*
☑ **write down** the names *them* of all the wedding guests
☑ **pick up** the wedding invitations

Using any of the two-word verbs in this chapter, practice this conversation with another student.

6.

☑ _____
☑ _____
☑ _____

respect 尊敬

I Heard from Him Just Last Week

hear from George	hear from him
~~hear George from~~	~~hear him from~~

A. Have you **heard from** your Uncle George recently?

B. Yes, I have. As a matter of fact, I **heard from** him just last week.*

*Or: the other day/a few days ago/a few minutes ago/ . . .

1. Have you **heard from** your cousin Betty recently?

her *Yes, I have.*

2. Have you **looked** *I have* **through** your old English book recently?

I look through it yesterday.

3. Have you **run into** Mr. Smith recently?

I run into him last week

4. Have you **gotten over** the flu yet?

I got over it last night

5. Has your English teacher **called on** you recently?

she have, She called me just last night

6. Have you been **picking on** your little brother lately?

I pick on him

Talk about some of the people in your life.
Do you have a good friend in another city? Who is he/she?
How often do you **hear from** him/her? How long have you known each other?
Who do you **get along with** very well? Why?
Who do you **take after**? How?
Who do you **look up to**? Why?

How about YOU?

I pick on him

A CHILD-REARING PROBLEM

Timmy and his little sister, Patty, don't get along with each other very well. In fact, they fight constantly. He picks on her when it's time for her to go to bed. She picks on him when his friends come over to play.

Timmy and Patty's parents are very concerned. They don't know what to do about their children. They have looked through several books on child rearing, but so far they can't seem to find an answer to the problem. They're hoping that eventually their children will learn to get along better with each other.

✔ CHECK-UP

True, False, or Maybe?

Answer True, False, or Maybe (if the answer isn't in the story).

1. Patty picks on Timmy when it's time for her to go to bed.
2. Timmy is Patty's older brother.
3. Timmy and Patty's parents have a child-rearing problem.
4. They can't seem to find any books about child rearing.
5. Timmy and Patty will eventually learn to get along better with each other.

Choose

1. Please don't _____ your little sister.
   a. pick on
   b. get along with

2. We've been _____ these old family pictures.
   a. looking through
   b. taking after

3. My teacher _____ me three times today.
   a. looked up to
   b. called on

4. I haven't _____ my aunt and uncle recently.
   a. gotten over
   b. heard from

5. I really _____ my older sister because she's so smart.
   a. run into
   b. look up to

6. Everybody thinks I _____ my mother.
   a. look through
   b. take after

7. I _____ my cousin Betty on Main Street yesterday.
   a. ran into
   b. heard from

8. Don't kiss me! I haven't _____ my cold yet.
   a. gotten along with
   b. gotten over

ON YOUR OWN: May I Help You?

You're looking for something in a department store. Complete this conversation and act it out with another student.

A. May I help you?

B. Yes, please. I'm **looking for** a ___*shoe*___ .

A. What size do you wear?

B. ___*small*___,* I think.

A. Here. How do you like (this one/these)?

B. Hmm. I think (it's/they're) a little too ___*bigger*___.† Do you have any ___*shoe*___s that are a little ___*small*___er?†

A. Yes. We have a wide selection. Why don't you **look through** all of our ___*shoe*___s on your own and **pick out** the (one/ones) you like?

B. Can I **try** (it/them) **on**?

A. Of course. You can **try** (it/them) **on** in the dressing room over there.

| *Size 32/34/36/ . . . | †fancy–plain |
| Small/Medium/Large/Extra Large | dark–light |

(5 minutes later)

A. Well, how (does it/do they) fit?

B. I'm afraid (it's/they're) a little too ___large___.* Do you have any ___raincoat___s that are a little ___small___er?*

A. Yes, we do. I think you'll like (THIS/THESE) ___raincoat___. (It's/They're) a little ___wide___er than the one(s) you just **tried on.**

B. Will you **take** (it/them) **back** if I decide to return (it/them)?

A. Of course. No problem at all. Just **bring** (it/them) **back** within ___7___ days, and we'll **give** you your money **back.**

B. Fine. I think I'll take (it/them). How much (does it/do they) cost?

A. The usual price is ___one hundred___dollars. But you're in luck! We're having a sale this week, and all of our ___rain coat___s are ___25 %___ percent off the regular price.

B. That's a real bargain! I'm glad I decided to buy (a)___raincoat___ this week. Thanks for your help.

A. My pleasure. Please come again.

> *large–small
> long –short
> wide –narrow
> tight –loose (baggy)

1. *raincoat*    2. *pair of gloves*    3. *sweater*   4.

ON SALE

Melvin went to a men's clothing store yesterday. He was looking for a new sports jacket. He looked through the entire selection of jackets and picked out a few that he really liked. First, he picked out a nice blue jacket. But when he tried it on, it was too small. Next, he picked out an attractive red jacket. But when he tried it on, it was too large. Finally, he picked out a very fancy brown jacket with gold buttons. And when he tried it on, it seemed to fit perfectly.

Then he decided to buy a pair of trousers to go with the jacket. He looked through the entire selection of trousers and picked out several pairs that he really liked. First, he picked out a light brown pair. But when he tried them on, they were too tight. Next, he picked out a dark brown pair. But when he tried them on, they were too loose. Finally, he picked out a pair of brown-and-white plaid pants. And when he tried them on, they seemed to fit perfectly.

Melvin paid for his new clothing and walked home feeling very happy about the jacket and pants he had just bought. He was especially happy because the clothing was on sale and he had paid 50 percent off the regular price.

However, Melvin's happiness didn't last very long. When he got home, he noticed that one arm of the jacket was longer than the other. He also realized very quickly that the zipper on the pants was broken.

The next day Melvin took the clothing back to the store and tried to get a refund. However, the people at the store refused to give him his money back because the clothing was on sale and there was a sign that said "ALL SALES ARE FINAL!"

Melvin was furious, but he knew he couldn't do anything about it. The next time he buys something on sale, he'll be more careful. And he'll be sure to read the signs!

✓CHECK-UP

What's the Sequence?

Put these sentences in the correct order, based on the story.

_____ But then, Melvin noticed problems with the jacket and the pants.
_____ Melvin picked out a few jackets he really liked.
_____ Melvin went back and asked for a refund.
_1_ Melvin went shopping for clothes yesterday.
_____ He walked home feeling very happy.
_____ He walked home feeling very upset and angry.
_____ The brown jacket seemed to fit perfectly.
_____ The store refused to give him back his money.
_____ A pair of plaid pants fit very well.
_____ He paid only half of the regular price.
_____ He picked out several pairs of trousers.

Listening

Listen and choose what the people are talking about.

1. a. an application form
   b. a math problem

2. a. shorts
   b. a blouse

3. a. shoes
   b. library books

4. a. homework
   b. children

5. a. pictures
   b. pants

6. a. the flu
   b. a decision

7. a. a coat
   b. the heat

8. a. milk
   b. the garbage

IN YOUR OWN WORDS

For Writing and Discussion

Have you ever bought anything that you had to return? Tell about it.

What did you buy?
Where?
What was wrong with it?
What did you do?
Were you successful?

CHAPTER 9 *SUMMARY*

GRAMMAR

Two-Word Verbs: Separable

I'm going to	**put on** my boots. **put** my boots **on.** **put** them **on.**

bring back the TV—**bring** it **back**	**put away** the clothes—**put** them **away**
call up Sally—**call** her **up**	**put on** your boots—**put** them **on**
clean up the living room—**clean** it **up**	**take back** the books—**take** them **back**
cross out the mistakes—**cross** them **out**	**take down** the decorations—**take** them **down**
do over the homework—**do** it **over**	**take off** your boots—**take** them **off**
drop off my sister—**drop** her **off**	**take out** the garbage—**take** it **out**
figure out the bill—**figure** it **out**	**think over** the decision—**think** it **over**
fill out the form—**fill** it **out**	**throw away** the notebook—**throw** it **away**
give back the ring—**give** it **back**	**throw out** the magazines—**throw** them **out**
hand in your homework—**hand** it **in**	**try on** the pants—**try** them **on**
hang up the portrait—**hang** it **up**	**turn down** the job offer—**turn** it **down**
look up the definition—**look** it **up**	**turn off** the oven—**turn** it **off**
pick out her gown—**pick** it **out**	**turn on** the heat—**turn** it **on**
pick up her clothes—**pick** them **up**	**write down** the number—**write** it **down**

Two-Word Verbs: Inseparable

I	**hear from** George **hear from** him ~~hear George from~~ ~~hear him from~~	very often.

call on	**look through**
get along with	**look up to**
get over	**pick on**
hear from	**run into**
look for	**take after**

FUNCTIONS

Extending an Invitation

Would you like to *go fishing this morning*?
Would you like to get together *today*?

Are you free *after you take them back*?

Declining an Invitation

I'd like to, but I can't.
I'd really like to, but I can't.
I'm afraid I can't.

Expressing Inability

I can't.
I'm afraid I can't.

Expressing Obligation

I have to *fill out my income tax form*.

I've really got to do it.

Asking for and Reporting Information

What size do you wear?
Size 32, I think.

How much *does it* cost?
The *usual* price is
_____ dollars.

Inquiring about Intention

Will you *take it back*?

When are you going to *call up your cousin*?

Expressing Intention

I'm going to *call him up next week*.
I'll *call you in the morning*.
I'll *turn it off* right away.

Inquiring about Remembering

Did you remember to *turn off the oven*?

Forgetting

I completely forgot!

Asking for Advice

Do you think I should *keep these old love letters*?

Offering Advice

I think you should *throw them away*.

Offering a Suggestion

Let's *get together tomorrow instead*.

Why don't you *look through all of our raincoats and pick out the one you like*?

Offering to Help

May I help you?

Expressing Want-Desire

I'm looking for *a raincoat*.

Do you have any *raincoats* that are *a little lighter*?

Connectors:
  And . . .Too ▪
  And . . . Either ▪
  So, But, Neither ▪

What a Coincidence!

I'm hungry.	I am, too. / So am I.
I can swim.	I can, too. / So can I.
I've seen that movie.	I have, too. / So have I.

I have a car.	I do, too. / So do I.
I worked yesterday.	I did, too. / So did I.

A. I'm allergic to cats.

B. What a coincidence!
{ I am, too. / So am I. }

1. I'm a vegetarian.

2. I like strawberry ice cream.

3. I can speak four languages fluently.

4. I just lost my job.

5. I'll be on vacation next week.

6. I've been feeling tired lately.

7. I have to work late at the office tonight.

8. I forgot to take my clothes off the clothes line this morning.

9.

What a Coincidence!

I'm not hungry. { I'm not either. / Neither am I. }

I can't swim. { I can't either. / Neither can I. }

I haven't seen that movie. { I haven't either. / Neither have I. }

I don't have a car. { I don't either. / Neither do I. }

I didn't work yesterday. { I didn't either. / Neither did I. }

A. I wasn't very athletic when I was younger.

B. What a coincidence! { I wasn't either. / Neither was I. }

1. I didn't see the stop sign.

2. I don't like war movies.

3. I'm not a very good tennis player.

4. I can't sing very well.

5. I've never kissed anyone before.

6. I don't drink coffee any more.

7. I won't be able to go bowling next Monday night.

8. I haven't prepared for today's lesson.

9.

121

And They Do, Too

I'm tired, { and he is, too. / and so is he. }

He'll be busy, { and she will, too. / and so will she. }

She's been sick, { and he has, too. / and so has he. }

They sing, { and she does, too. / and so does she. }

She studied, { and I did, too. / and so did I. }

A. Why can't you or the children help me with the dishes?

B. I have to study, { **and they do, too.** / **and so do they.** }

1. **A.** Why are you and your brother so tired?
   B. I stayed up late last night, _____.

2. **A.** What are you and your girlfriend going to do tomorrow?
   B. I'm going to study at the library, _____.

3. **A.** Why are you and Gloria so nervous?
   B. She has an English exam tomorrow, _____.

4. **A.** Where were you and your husband when the accident happened?
   B. I was standing on the corner, _____.

5. **A.** Why can't you or Dr. Johnson see me next Monday?

   B. I'll be out of town, _____.

7. **A.** How do you know Mr. and Mrs. Jenkins?

   B. They sing in the church choir, _____.

9. **A.** Why don't you or your neighbors complain about this broken door?

   B. I've already spoken to the landlord, _____.

11. **A.** Why are you and your cats hiding under the bed?

    B. I'm afraid of thunder and lightning, _____.

13. **A.** Why are you in love with Robert?

    B. I appreciate literature, music, and other beautiful things, _____.

6. **A.** Why haven't you and your sister been in school for the past few days?

   B. I've been sick, _____.

8. **A.** Could you or your friend help me take these packages upstairs?

   B. I'll be glad to help you, _____.

10. **A.** How did you meet your wife?

    B. I was washing clothes at the laundromat one day, _____.

12. **A.** What are you two arguing about?

    B. He wants this parking space, _____.

14.

MADE FOR EACH OTHER

Louise and Brian are very compatible people. They have a lot in common. For example, they have very similar backgrounds. He grew up in a small town in the South, and so did she. She's the oldest of four children, and he is, too. His parents own their own business, and so do hers.

They also have similar academic interests. She's majoring in Chemistry, and he is, too. He has taken every course in Mathematics offered by their college, and so has she. She enjoys working with computers, and he does, too.

In addition, Louise and Brian like the same sports. He goes swimming several times a week, and so does she. She can play tennis very well, and so can he. His favorite winter sport is ice skating, and hers is, too.

Louise and Brian also have the same cultural interests. She has been to most of the art museums in New York City, and so has he. He's a member of the college theater group, and she is, too. She has a complete collection of Beethoven's symphonies, and so does he.

In addition, they have very similar personalities. She has always been very shy, and he has, too. He tends to be very quiet, and so does she. She's often nervous when she's in large groups of people, and he is, too.

Finally, they have very similar outlooks on life. She has been a vegetarian for years, and so has he. He supports equal rights for women and minorities, and so does she. She's opposed to the use of nuclear energy, and he is, too.

As you can see, Louise and Brian are very compatible people. In fact, everybody says they were "made for each other."

 CHECK-UP

True, False, or Maybe?

Answer True, False, or Maybe (if the answer isn't in the story).

1. Brian doesn't have any older brothers or sisters.
2. Louise and Brian are both students in college.
3. They both ski very well.
4. They haven't been to all the art museums in New York City.
5. They both feel that people shouldn't eat vegetables.

Listening

Listen and choose what the people are talking about.

1. a. personality
   b. background

2. a. sports
   b. cultural interests

3. a. academic interests
   b. outlook on life

4. a. personality
   b. background

5. a. cultural interests
   b. outlook on life

And He Can't Either

I'm not tired, { and he isn't either. / and neither is he. }

He won't be busy, { and she won't either. / and neither will she. }

She hasn't been sick, { and he hasn't either. / and neither has he. }

They don't sing, { and she doesn't either. / and neither does she. }

She didn't study, { and I didn't either. / and neither did I. }

A. Why do you and your husband want to enroll in my dance class?

B. I can't dance the cha cha or the fox trot, { **and he can't either.** / **and neither can he.** }

1. **A.** Why do you and William look so confused?

   B. I don't understand today's grammar, _____.

2. **A.** Why didn't you or your parents answer the telephone all weekend?

   B. I wasn't home, _____.

3. **A.** Why do you and your roommate have to move?

   B. He didn't have enough money to pay the rent this month, _____.

4. **A.** Why do you and your sister look so frightened?

   B. I've never been on a roller coaster before, _____.

5. **A.** Why are you and your friends so late?

    B. I couldn't remember your address, _____.

6. **A.** What do you and Fred want to talk to me about?

    B. I won't be able to come to work tomorrow, _____.

7. **A.** Why don't you and your friends want to come to the ballgame?

    B. They aren't very interested in baseball, _____.

8. **A.** Why does the school nurse want to see us?

    B. I haven't had a flu shot yet, _____.

9. **A.** What are you and your sister arguing about?

    B. She doesn't want to take the garbage out, _____.

10. **A.** Why didn't you or Mom wake us up on time this morning?

    B. I didn't hear the alarm clock, _____.

11. **A.** Why were you and your wife so nervous during the flight?

    B. I had never flown before today, _____.

12. **A.** Why have you and your friends stopped shopping at my store?

    B. I can't afford your prices, _____.

13. **A.** Why don't you and your little sister want me to read *Little Red Riding Hood*?

    B. I don't like fairy tales very much, _____.

14.

LAID OFF

Jack and Betty Williams are going through some difficult times. They were both laid off from their jobs last month. As the days go by, they're becoming more and more concerned about their futures, since he hasn't been able to find another job yet, and neither has she.

The layoffs weren't a surprise to Jack and Betty. After all, Jack's company hadn't been doing very well for a long time, and neither had Betty's. However, Jack had never expected both of them to be laid off at the same time, and Betty hadn't either. Ever since they have been laid off, Jack and Betty have been trying to find new jobs. Unfortunately, she hasn't been very successful, and he hasn't either.

The main reason they're having trouble finding work is that there simply aren't many jobs available right now. He can't find anything in the want ads, and neither can she. She hasn't heard about any job openings, and he hasn't either. His friends haven't been able to help at all, and neither have hers.

Another reason they're having trouble finding work is that they don't seem to have the right kind of skills and training. He doesn't know anything about computers, and she doesn't either. She can't type very well, and neither can he. He hasn't had any special vocational training, and she hasn't either.

A third reason they're having trouble finding work is that there are certain jobs they prefer not to take. He doesn't like working at night, and neither does she. She isn't willing to work on the weekends, and neither is he. He doesn't want to commute very far to work, and she doesn't either.

Despite all their problems, Jack and Betty aren't completely discouraged. She doesn't have a very pessimistic outlook on life, and neither does he. They're both hopeful that things will get better soon.

✔CHECK-UP

True, False, or Maybe?

Answer True, False, or Maybe (if the answer isn't in the story).

1. Jack quit his job last month.
2. Jack and Betty had been working for the same company.
3. Some of their friends have been laid off, too.
4. Typing skills are important in certain jobs.
5. Jack and Betty will find jobs soon.

A Job Interview

You're at a job interview. Role play with another student, using the interviewer's questions below.

Tell me about your skills.
Tell me about your educational background.
Have you had any special vocational training?
Are you willing to work at night or on weekends?
When can you start?

Why Don't You Ask Them?

I don't sing, but my sister does.
She didn't know the answer, but I did.
He can play chess, but I can't.
We're ready, but they aren't.

A. Do you know the answer to question number 9?

B. No, I don't, but **Charles** does. Why don't you ask him?

1. Do you have a hammer?
my upstairs neighbors

2. Are you interested in seeing a movie tonight?
Bob

3. Can you baby-sit for us tomorrow night?
my sister

4. Have you heard tomorrow's weather forecast?
my father

5. Did you write down the homework assignment?
Maria

6. Do you want to go dancing tonight?
Julia

7. Have you by any chance found a brown-and-white dog?
the people across the street

8. Were you paying attention when the salesman explained how to put together this toy?
the children

TOUCHY SUBJECTS

Larry and his parents never agree when they talk about politics. Larry is very liberal, but his parents aren't. They're very conservative. Larry thinks the President is doing a very poor job, but his parents don't. They think the President is doing a fine job. Also, Larry doesn't think the government should spend a lot of money on defense, but his parents do. They think the country needs a strong army. You can see why Larry and his parents never agree when they talk about politics. Politics is a very "touchy subject" with them.

The Greens and their next-door neighbors, the Harrisons, never agree when they talk about child rearing. The Greens are very lenient with their children, but the Harrisons aren't. They're very strict. The Greens let their children watch television whenever they want, but the Harrisons don't. They let their children watch television for only an hour a day. Also, the Harrisons have always taught their children to sit quietly and behave well at the dinner table, but the Greens haven't. They have always allowed their children to do whatever they want at the dinner table. You can see why the Greens and their next-door neighbors, the Harrisons, never agree when they talk about child rearing. Child rearing is a very "touchy subject" with them.

✔CHECK-UP

True or False?

1. Larry and his parents always disagree when they talk about politics.
2. Larry probably supports equal rights for women and minorities.
3. The Harrisons' children watch television more often than the Greens' children.
4. The Greens' children probably go to bed later than the Harrisons' children.
5. Since the Greens and the Harrisons disagree, they never talk about child rearing.

IN YOUR OWN WORDS

For Writing and Discussion

Tell a story about a "touchy subject" between you and another person.

Who is the person?
What do you disagree about?
In what ways do you disagree?
(Use "I _____, but _____" in your story.)

ON YOUR OWN: Same and Different

In many ways, my brother and I are exactly the same:
  I'm tall and thin, and he is, too.
  I have brown eyes and black curly hair, and so does he.
  I work in an office downtown, and he does, too.
  I'm not married yet, and neither is he.
  I went to college in Boston, and so did he.
  I wasn't a very good student, and he wasn't either.

And in many ways, my brother and I are very different:
  I like classical music, but he doesn't.
  He enjoys sports, but I don't.
  I've never traveled overseas, but he has.
  He's never been to New York, but I have many times.
  He's very outgoing and popular, but I'm not.
  I'm very quiet and philosophical, but he isn't.

Yes, in many ways, my brother and I are exactly the same, and in many ways, we're very different. But most important of all, we like and respect each other. And we're friends.

Compare yourself with somebody you are close to: a friend, a classmate, or somebody in your family.

In many ways, _____ and I are exactly the same:

_____

_____

_____

_____

And in many ways, _____ and I are very different:

_____

_____

_____

_____

GRAMMAR

Connectors
Too/So

I'm hungry.	I am, too. So am I.
I can swim.	I can, too. So can I.
I've seen that movie.	I have, too. So have I.
I have a car.	I do, too. So do I.
I worked yesterday.	I did, too. So did I.

Either/Neither

I'm not hungry.	I'm not either. Neither am I.
I can't swim.	I can't either. Neither can I.
I haven't seen that movie.	I haven't either. Neither have I.
I don't have a car.	I don't either. Neither do I.
I didn't work.	I didn't either. Neither did I.

But

I don't sing, **but** my sister does.	

I'm tired,	and he is, too. and so is he.
He'll be busy,	and she will, too. and so will she.
She's been sick,	and he has, too. and so has he.
They sing,	and she does, too. and so does she.
She studied,	and I did, too. and so did I.

I'm not tired,	and he isn't either. and neither is he.
He won't be busy,	and she won't either. and neither will she.
She hasn't been sick,	and he hasn't either. and neither has he.
They don't sing,	and she doesn't either. and neither does she.
She didn't study,	and I didn't either. and neither did I.

FUNCTIONS

Asking for and Reporting Information

Do you know *the answer to question number 9*?

How do you know *Mr. and Mrs. Jenkins*?

Have you heard *tomorrow's weather forecast*?

Where were you when *the accident happened*?
I was *standing on the corner*.

Tell me about your *skills*.
Have you had *any special vocational training*?
When can you *start*?

Expressing Likes

I like *strawberry ice cream*.

I appreciate *literature, music, and other beautiful things*.

He enjoys *sports*.

Expressing Dislikes

I don't like *war movies*.
I don't like *fairy tales* very much.

Inquiring about Want-Desire

Why do *you and your husband* want to *enroll in my dance class*?

What *do you and Fred* want to *talk to me about*?

Why don't *you and your friends* want to *come to the ballgame*?

Expressing Want-Desire

He wants *this parking space*.

She doesn't want to *take the garbage out*.

Inquiring about Ability

Can you *baby-sit for us tomorrow night*?

Expressing Ability

I can *speak four languages fluently*.

Expressing Inability

I'm not a very good *tennis player*.

I can't *dance the cha cha*.
I can't *sing* very well.

I won't be able to *go bowling next Monday night*.

Inquiring about Intention

What *are you and your girlfriend* going to do *tomorrow*?

Expressing Intention

I'm going to *study at the library*.

Extending an Invitation

Are you interested in *seeing a movie tonight*?
Do you want to *go dancing tonight*?

Describing

My brother and I are exactly the same.
My brother and I are very different.

I'm tall and thin.
I have *brown eyes and black curly hair*.
He's very *outgoing and popular*.

Inquiring about Feelings-Emotions

Why do *you and your sister* look so frightened?

Why were *you and your wife* so nervous?

APPENDIX

Irregular Verbs

be	was	been	leave	left	left
become	became	become	lend	lent	lent
begin	began	begun	let	let	let
bite	bit	bitten	light	lit	lit
blow	blew	blown	lose	lost	lost
break	broke	broken	make	made	made
bring	brought	brought	mean	meant	meant
build	built	built	meet	met	met
buy	bought	bought	put	put	put
catch	caught	caught	quit	quit	quit
choose	chose	chosen	read	read	read
come	came	come	ride	rode	ridden
cost	cost	cost	ring	rang	rung
cut	cut	cut	run	ran	run
do	did	done	say	said	said
draw	drew	drawn	see	saw	seen
drink	drank	drunk	sell	sold	sold
drive	drove	driven	send	sent	sent
eat	ate	eaten	set	set	set
fall	fell	fallen	sew	sewed	sewed/sewn
feed	fed	fed	shake	shook	shaken
feel	felt	felt	shrink	shrank	shrunk
fight	fought	fought	sing	sang	sung
find	found	found	sit	sat	sat
fit	fit	fit	sleep	slept	slept
fly	flew	flown	speak	spoke	spoken
forget	forgot	forgotten	spend	spent	spent
forgive	forgave	forgiven	stand	stood	stood
freeze	froze	frozen	steal	stole	stolen
get	got	gotten	sweep	swept	swept
give	gave	given	swim	swam	swum
go	went	gone	take	took	taken
grow	grew	grown	teach	taught	taught
hang	hung	hung	tell	told	told
have	had	had	think	thought	thought
hear	heard	heard	throw	threw	thrown
hide	hid	hidden	understand	understood	understood
hit	hit	hit	wake	woke	woken
hold	held	held	wear	wore	worn
hurt	hurt	hurt	win	won	won
keep	kept	kept	wind	wound	wound
know	knew	known	write	wrote	written
lead	led	led			

Tape Scripts for Listening Exercises

Chapter 1 – p. 6

Listen and choose the best answer.

1. What are you doing?
2. Do you swim very often?
3. Are you a good cook?
4. What's Tom cooking?
5. Who cooks in your family?
6. Do they like to study?
7. Does he want to be a violinist?
8. Are you and your brother busy this afternoon?
9. Does Mrs. King like to swim?
10. What's Peter reading?

Chapter 2 – p. 18

Listen and choose the best answer.

1. Did you do well at your job interview yesterday?
2. What did your children do this morning?
3. What was she doing when she broke her arm?
4. What was his supervisor doing?
5. Sally, why did you fall asleep during class?
6. Why didn't you finish your dinner?
7. What happened while he was jogging in the park?
8. Did you do well on your exam?
9. Were you looking for an apartment all day yesterday?
10. Were demonstrators shouting while the President was speaking?

Chapter 3 – p. 26

Listen to the conversation and choose the answer that is true.

1. A. Don't wear your blue suit tonight. You wore it last weekend.
   B. All right. Where's my BLACK suit?
2. A. Do we need anything from the supermarket?
   B. Yes. We need some beef, some potatoes, and some tomatoes.
3. A. Which movie do you want to see?
   B. How about "The Man in the Brown Suit"?
   A. Okay. What channel is it on?
4. A. What are you going to do tomorrow?
   B. I'm going to plant lettuce, tomatoes, and beans.
5. A. What's the matter with it?
   B. The brakes don't work, and it doesn't start very well in the morning.
6. A. This car is very nice, but it's too expensive.
   B. You're right.

Chapter 4 – p. 45

1. *Sharon is on vacation in San Francisco. She's checking her list of things to do while she's on vacation. On the list below, check the things Sharon has already done.*

   Sharon has already seen the Golden Gate Bridge. She hasn't visited Golden Gate Park yet. She took a tour of Alcatraz Prison yesterday. She's going to go to Chinatown tomorrow. She's eaten at Fisherman's Wharf, and she hasn't had time to buy souvenirs yet.

2. *Alan is a secretary in a very busy office. He's checking his list of things to do before 5 P.M. on Friday. On the list below, check the things Alan has already done.*

   Alan has called Mrs. Porter. He has to type the letter to the Ajax Insurance Company. He's gone to the bank. He hasn't taken the mail to the post office. He cleaned the coffee machine, and he's going to speak to the boss about his salary.

3. *It's Saturday, and Judy and Paul Johnson are doing lots of things around the house. They're checking the list of things they have to do today. On the list below, check the things they've already done.*

   Judy and Paul haven't done the laundry. They have to wash the kitchen windows. They've paid the bills. They'll clean the garage later. They couldn't fix the bathroom sink, but they vacuumed the living room.

Chapter 5 – p. 56

Listen to the conversation and choose the answer that is true.

1. A. How long have you had a toothache?
   B. For three days.
2. A. How long was your knee swollen?
   B. For a week.
3. A. Has your father always been an engineer?
   B. No, he hasn't.
4. A. How long have you known how to skate?
   B. Since I was a teenager.
5. A. Did you live in Rome for a long time?
   B. Yes. Five years.
6. A. How long has Jim been interested in Greek literature?
   B. Since he lived in Greece.

7. A. Is Betty still in the hospital?
   B. Oh, I forgot to tell you. She's been home for two days.
8. A. Have you liked country music for a long time?
   B. Yes. I've liked country music since I moved to Nashville seven years ago.

Chapter 6 – p. 71

I. Listen and decide who is speaking.

1. What a day! All day the tenants have been complaining that nothing is working.
2. I'm very tired. I've given six lessons today.
3. It's been a long day. I've been selling tickets since ten A.M.
4. I'm really tired. I've been watching them all day.
5. Thank you! You've been a wonderful audience!
6. I'm exhausted! I've been looking at paychecks since early this morning.

II. Listen and choose the word you hear.

1. She's gone to sleep.
2. I've never written so many letters in one day before.
3. I've been seeing patients all day.
4. What courses have you taken this year?
5. Is Henry giving blood?
6. Ben has driven all night.

Chapter 7 – p. 85

Listen and choose the best answer.

1. A. I avoid driving downtown whenever I can.
   B. Me, too.
2. A. I've decided to sell my car.
   B. Your beautiful car?
3. A. Please try to quit biting your nails.
   B. Okay, Mom.
4. A. We're thinking about moving to California.
   B. Oh. That's interesting.
5. A. I've been considering getting married for a long time.
   B. Oh, really? I didn't know that.
6. A. Don't stop practicing!
   B. Okay.

Chapter 8 – p. 95

Listen and choose the best answer.

1. I hadn't seen that movie before.
2. I haven't gone swimming in years.
3. Has the play started yet?
4. Michael, please go upstairs and do your homework!
5. Why did Carmen do well on the History test?
6. I enjoyed dinner at Stanley's Restaurant last night.

Chapter 9 – p. 108

Listen and write the missing words.

Dear Alice,

I'm very discouraged. I'm having a lot of trouble with my girlfriend and I don't know what to do. The problem is very simple: I'm in love with her, but she isn't in love with me! A few weeks ago, I gave her a ring, but she gave it back. During the past few months I have written several love letters to her, but she has thrown them away. Recently I asked her to marry me. She thought it over for a while, and then she turned me down. Now when I try to call her up she doesn't even want to talk to me. Please try to help me. I don't know what to do.

"Discouraged Donald"
Denver, Colorado

Chapter 9 – p. 117

Listen and choose what the people are talking about.

1. A. Have you filled it out yet?
   B. No, I'm having some trouble. Can you help me?
2. A. Where can I try them on?
   B. The dressing room is right over there.
3. A. Now remember, you can't bring them back!
   B. I understand.
4. A. Please drop them off at the school by eight o'clock.
   B. By eight o'clock? Okay.
5. A. Where should I hang them up?
   B. What about over the fireplace?
6. A. Have you thought it over?
   B. Yes, I have.
7. A. It's cold in here.
   B. You're right. I'll turn it on.
8. A. Should we use it up?
   B. No, let's throw it out.

Chapter 10 – p. 125

Listen and choose what the people are talking about.

1. A. To tell the truth, I'm a little shy.
   B. What a coincidence! I am, too.
2. A. I enjoy going to plays and concerts.
   B. We're very compatible. So do I.
3. A. I'm enjoying this course.
   B. I am, too.
4. A. I'm from Minnesota.
   B. That's interesting. So am I.
5. A. I'm opposed to using animals in scientific experiments.
   B. I am, too.

Glossary

The number after each word indicates the page where the word first appears. Words introduced in Books 1 and 2 are not included in this list.
(adj) = adjective, (adv) = adverb, (n) = noun, (v) = verb

A

a little later **29**
a little while **27**
a long time **27**
a lot **13**
academic **124**
accent **55**
accept **107**
accident report **105**
accidentally **108**
accomplish **100**
advise **70**
aerobics **3**
afford **127**
ahead of time **90**
airplane **68**
alarm clock **127**
Algebra **111**
all right **65**
allergic (to) **120**
allow **130**
already **36**
ankle **96**
answer (n) **113**
apparently **108**
appreciate **78**
argue **8**
army **8**
art **53**
as soon as **65**
aspirin **38**
assemble **71**
assignment **129**
assistant manager **57**
astronaut **55**
astronomy **49**
at the back (of) **16**
at this point **38**
audience **16**
available **128**
avoid **76**

B

baby-sit **129**
baby-sitter **71**
bachelor **56**
background **124**

baggy **115**
balcony **94**
ballet dancer **5**
barber **58**
beard **81**
been **48**
Beethoven **2**
beforehand **101**
beginning (n) **38**
behave **130**
behind **16**
best friend **15**
bet (v) **17**
bill **8**
Bingo **37**
black and blue **50**
black eye **15**
boat **19**
body **50**
bone **97**
bookkeeper **42**
bother **70**
bottom **57**
box (v) **79**
break up **99**
bridge **63**
bring along **90**
bring back **104**
bump into **94**
button **116**

C

call back **29**
call on **112**
call up **105**
camping **26**
cancel **99**
canoeing **88**
carpenter **54**
cashier **55**
ceiling **65**
ceremony **101**
certain **128**
cha cha **126**
Channel *2* **25**
check (v) **108**
Chemistry **69**
chess match **98**

chew **97**
child rearing **113**
childhood **94**
choir **93**
Christmas decorations **111**
Christmas present **67**
church choir **123**
clean up **110**
cleaners **104**
clerk **57**
clothing **20**
coach (n) **5**
coincidence **120**
collection **124**
college application
  form **104**
Colorado **108**
Colosseum **20**
come back **30**
come home **21**
commute (v) **128**
compatible **124**
compose **2**
composition **32**
computer technology **49**
confused **126**
conservative **130**
consider **80**
constantly **113**
continue **82**
cook (n) **4**
corporation **57**
correct (adj) **108**
costume **91**
count (v) **53**
course **89**
cover (v) **13**
co-worker **42**
critical **77**
cross out **107**
cultural **124**
curtain **91**

D

daily **15**
daily exercises **15**
dance ballet (v) **5**
dance class **126**

dance teacher **5**
day off **33**
decision **80**
decorations **111**
dedicated (adj) **50**
defense **130**
definition **107**
Democrats **54**
demonstrator **16**
Denver **108**
department **57**
deserve **100**
desk **42**
despite **128**
dinner party **90**
dinner table **89**
discouraged (adj) **108**
discuss **89**
dizzy **50**
do *her* food shopping **37**
do over **107**
do poorly **99**
doorbell **90**
draw **79**
dressing room **114**
driver's manual **100**
driver's test **40**
driveway **90**
driving school **100**
drop off **109**

E

earn **100**
eat out **88**
educational background **128**
electric bill **8**
emotional **30**
Empire State Building **45**
end (n) **91**
energy **125**
engaged **52**
engineer **56**
engineering **83**
enroll **83**
envy (v) **78**
equal **125**
equal rights **125**
erase **107**

Expressions

short.   long.

ɛ   e.

ʌ   a

INDEX